RUHE BAYORS

BALBOA.PRESS
A DIVISION OF HAY HOUSE

Copyright © 2020 Ruhe Bayors.

All rights reserved. No part of this book may be used or reproduced by any means, graphic, electronic, or mechanical, including photocopying, recording, taping or by any information storage retrieval system without the written permission of the author except in the case of brief quotations embodied in critical articles and reviews.

Balboa Press books may be ordered through booksellers or by contacting:

Balboa Press
A Division of Hay House
1663 Liberty Drive
Bloomington, IN 47403
www.balboapress.com
1 (877) 407-4847

Because of the dynamic nature of the Internet, any web addresses or links contained in this book may have changed since publication and may no longer be valid. The views expressed in this work are solely those of the author and do not necessarily reflect the views of the publisher, and the publisher hereby disclaims any responsibility for them.

The author of this book does not dispense medical advice or prescribe the use of any technique as a form of treatment for physical, emotional, or medical problems without the advice of a physician, either directly or indirectly. The intent of the author is only to offer information of a general nature to help you in your quest for emotional and spiritual well-being. In the event you use any of the information in this book for yourself, which is your constitutional right, the author and the publisher assume no responsibility for your actions.

Any people depicted in stock imagery provided by Getty Images are models, and such images are being used for illustrative purposes only. Certain stock imagery © Getty Images.

Print information available on the last page.

ISBN: 978-1-9822-3890-2 (sc)
ISBN: 978-1-9822-3892-6 (hc)
ISBN: 978-1-9822-3891-9 (e)

Balboa Press rev. date: 12/27/2019

Contents

Dedicated ix

1	And so the Journey Begins…	1
2	Synchronicity	5
3	Showers of Blessings	9
4	So, you want to see a miracle?	11
5	Guardianship	15
6	The Thanksgiving Table	17
7	Joy	21
8	Why Gardening?	25
9	Hokey Pokey	29
10	Going Deep	33
11	Amen	37
12	Chaos	41
13	Spring	45
14	This Singular Journey	49
15	Hallelujah!	51
16	God is Not One Religion	55
17	Rainbow Bridges and Doggie Doors	59
18	To Everything There is a Season	63
19	Maranatha Park and Broadway	67
20	Namaste	71
21	The Plight of the Slightly Enlightened	75
22	The Pareto Principle	79
23	A Thousand Forks	83
24	Come Home	87
25	Your Garden Wall	91
26	Heart of Hearts	93
27	Golden Calf	97
28	The Foolish Gardener	99
29	Ignite a Fire in Your Soul	103
30	The Importance of Roots	107

31	The Cleansing	109
32	Thanksgiving	111
33	Why I Lied to My Minister	113
34	Merry Christmas	117
35	Christmas Eve	119
36	It Is a New Year!	123
37	Belief in God	125
38	The Seeds of Desire	129
39	Everlasting Love	133
40	Beyond the Five Senses	135
41	God is Limitless	137
42	Billy	139
43	Last Words	143
44	Confirmation Bias	147
45	A New Hope	151
46	Springtime	153
47	Take My Hand	155
48	Embracing God	157
49	It's All a Mystery	161
50	The Wakeup Call	165
51	"I Don't Know How to Love Him"	167
52	Inside Out	171
53	Bible Stories	175
54	"Some Things are True"	179
55	The Greatest Illusionist	183
56	Sabbath	187
57	I Want Kindness	191
58	Horatio	195
59	"For God So Loved the World"	199
60	Spiritual Anxiety	203
61	Shift Happens	207
62	What's In a Name?	211
63	Knock, Knock	215
64	Repeat After Me	219
65	Broken Record	223

66	Feeding Your Soul	225
67	It's the Holiday Season	227
68	Anticipation	231
69	Where are you Christmas?	235
70	What's Missing?	239
71	"Tis the Season	241
72	I Surrender All	245
73	WYSIWYG	247
74	So Many Paths	251
75	The Devil is in the Detail	255
76	Potholes on the Road to Enlightenment	259
77	How Deep is Your Love?	263
78	Finding Your Sweet Spot	267
79	Holier Than Thou	271
80	Bible Warfare	275
81	Spring Cleaning	279
82	Peace	283
83	Surrounded	287
84	Tithes and Offerings	289
85	Here and Now	291
86	Oh, Happy Day!	295
87	God Did It	299
88	Providence	303
89	Seeing With Spiritual Eyes	307
90	Choosing to Live with a Spiritual Heart	311
91	Erring on the Side of Love	315
92	Jesus or Nothing	319
93	Why Now, Lord?	321
94	Spiritual Hunger	323
95	You, Radical You!	325
96	What is Your Philosophy?	329
97	The Night is Magic	331
98	True North	333
99	Cruising the River Denial	337
100	Kintsugi	341

101	Open Sesame	343
102	The Pursuit of Happiness	347
103	Full Embrace	349
104	Shaping the Future	351
105	God Helps Those	355
106	Of Square Pegs and Round Holes	359

Endnotes 363

Dedicated

To my maternal grandparents who exhibited

every beautiful aspect of

loving our Lord

With special appreciation to 'The Soph'

1

And so the Journey Begins...

⁂

Soul Gardening has been a dream of mine for a very long time, but suddenly, this was the most important thing on my agenda. That is all because of a little dog named Sophie, who belongs to a dear friend of mine. Because of Sophie, I made a promise to God to write this book, and, of course, I had to keep that promise.

Now you should know it was because of 'The Soph' that I got my own little dog, Tucker, a few months later. They were cousins, and two of the greatest joys of our lives.

My friend and I went to a concert one night in another city, so Sophie, along with my two dogs and a cat, went to a pet boarding facility for an overnight stay. That was three years ago now, and it is where this tale begins. For when we went to pick them up the next day, Sophie was nowhere to be found.

No one quite knew what to do, as a mix-up like this had never happened before. So, everyone panicked! The owner rifled through the records of the day and focused on which small dogs resembling Sophie were released to what owners. There was a lot of scrambling around, and the looks of alarm on everyone's faces brought no comfort to us as we were forced to stand there amid it all. The anxiety was palpable, and tears started to well up.

I decided to take my critters home, as my menagerie was creating a massive bottleneck in the small lobby. Promising my friend to return as soon as possible and wait with her until Sophie was returned unscathed. As I drove the short distance to my home, I boldly told God I needed to call in a favor. As if He owed me anything! But I told Him I desperately needed 'The Soph' to be found and returned to my friend. Sophie had always been a very special dog with a charismatic personality. She was bonded closely to my friend, and they both needed each other.

In return, I promised to write a book for Him that spoke of my experiences and my devotion.

Now, keep in mind, if anything I had only played at writing. Oh, I wrote things in my business life, perhaps a manual or two. I had had longings to write books, and even submitted a couple chapters to an agent once. Honestly, I think that agent is still chuckling about that submission. But a book about God? What was I thinking? Not that I was thinking at the time. I believed it was the only way I could help to get Sophie back.

By the time I had returned to the boarding facility, the owner had located Sophie less than a mile away. The elderly owners of another dog still at the facility, had not even noticed that the dog they took home was a little female, and not the boy they had boarded.

Everyone finally relieved, and all doggies with the correct owners, I had some writing to do. God answered my prayers by fulfilling my request for a favor, it was the very least I could do.

Sophie is still a big part my life, visiting regularly. I love her dearly and will never forget that she is the one who initiated this Soul Gardening journey.

Soul Gardening is about believing that our spirit will thrive if we tend to it as we would a garden. As the seasons change over the course of these few years, so do the stories. Soul gardeners of all experience levels are welcome to share in my faith, my prayers, and my love for the Lord.

We will discuss being watchful and protective, so our Soul Garden grows and thrives. We will discover how to limit, as much as possible, the harshness that nature can provide, understanding that fears and storms are a part of life. We will learn how to pay attention to our beliefs and values, seeking to understand and mitigate the conflict that comes from digging into our spiritual roots.

Upkeep is tremendously important for any garden and remembering to feel gratitude for every experience helps to provide that. This is also the time when we eagerly watch for miracles all around us.

Even a very proficient soul gardener, who knows how to make hope and joy flow, should enjoy the reminders to cherish each moment, and always communicate with the Creator.

So, celebrate along with me, as I ask many questions, search for answers, and try to figure out what we truly want to believe and value. Happy to have you along for the ride.

And so, it begins. Blessings!

2

Synchronicity

⋙ ⋘

Nurturing our relationship with the Divine is a major component of spiritual practice. We can talk to God all day long. We can pray all night long. We chat, we ask, we plead. We can have a private conversation with Him in our heads, if we choose. How is the other side of that relationship revealed though? Where is the correlation to all this chatter coming from the human side of this connection?

I do not hear a booming voice advising me what to do, nor do visions appear to guide me like a movie. However, I do try to pay attention and listen to what is going on around me. And Lord, I know you are hearing my prayers. I would rather respond to one of Your whispers than get hit on the head with a 2x4 because I was not paying attention.

Is this one of God's whispers?

Bicycles have been a part of my life since I was barely able to walk. I love them. I have had and ridden every kind of bicycle imaginable: cruisers, road, and mountain. You name it. Even a professional racing model once. I am a sucker for all of them.

As we all know, life happens, priorities shift, and bicycle

riding just drifted away from me. Close to ten years went by with me not owning a two-wheeled pleasure machine. The spark that was going to bring this all back to me was my city council voting to build a bike path behind my home.

This was unbelievable, and a perfect opportunity I thought to get back into it. That, along with the gorgeous spring weather, really got me going, and before long I was going on test rides offered by local bike shops, searching the Internet, talking to friends. The hunt was on.

And suddenly there she was: a magnificent candy apple red hybrid bicycle. I was smitten and felt like a little kid in a candy store. After a test ride, I thought a longer seat post would make the fit perfect, but the salesman said, no, it would be better to get you the next larger frame. It should only take about three weeks to get it ordered. One hundred dollars down, a receipt in hand, and a smile on my face...Life was looking good. The weather was just a tease. Dazzling warm, sunny days with temperate mornings and evenings.

An extended business trip came up at the end of week three, so I waited to call the shop for an update. Anxiously checking email every day – where is my ride? Finally, home at last, the first stop I made was...the bicycle store. Greeted this time by the owner, I presented my order only to be told, "We didn't order that, it doesn't come in that frame size."

You have got to be kidding me? I waited how long, and no one called to tell me? He continued...we can change the seat post...yada yada...on the bike you already tested... yada yada...but we will have to order a new one because the one you tried out has been sold. I felt deceived, and as disappointed as a child on Christmas morning not getting what I had really wanted.

Sorry, but no. The joy I had felt was extinguished. It was a betrayal, not only by the bike store, but also now by the weather. The perfect spring had transformed in that short period of time into a hot, dry, sauna topping one hundred degrees daily. No. The dreams of long, gentle rides into the sunset had dissipated. No. I would need my hundred dollars back, please. Thank you.

The summer parched away my need for a shiny new toy. But six months later, autumn's cooler days called me to spend more time outside. Another urge to ride, another yearning for the great outdoors, another search, and then another find. This time a stunning purple beauty. A bit more expensive, so thought it a sensible idea to sleep on the decision. Tomorrow morning will dictate how to proceed.

Big deep breath on arising. Yes, I will move forward. I open my laptop to national news that this morning the CEO of a large company was riding her bicycle on a road a few miles outside of the city, and very close to where I used to ride every weekend. A car knocked her down, killing her. No, this cannot be.

Why did I hear this today of all days? Was this a sign? A hint? Dare I say a whisper? Well, I just could not place that order. The thought of doing that just did not sit right. I'd never considered that anything bad could happen on a bicycle.

Two more seasons pass, back to the joy of spring, and no surprise, the bicycle bug is biting yet again. Back to research mode. You know the drill by now. And red is again my color of choice. Big expense for the new choice. More expensive each time. Sleep on it, I tell myself. What could it hurt?

Morning comes after dreaming of bike rides across Europe. Laptop fired up. Local news this time. (By now you have got to be thinking this is all made up...It is not.) A gentleman, father of two, enjoying an early morning bike ride on the street a friend of mine lives on, was struck and killed by another father driving a minivan. Apparently, the sunrise blinded the driver, and he could not see the cyclist. This cannot be happening again.

Okay, so now I have got to wonder how my buying and riding a bicycle is correlated to all these happenings. No, seriously, what is happening here?

Needless to say, I cannot order this bicycle either.

Time heals, and so another season, another urge. Dozens of people now using the bike path next to my house. They are all, of course, having a great time! We are about five months out now from the last purchasing debacle. By now I am on every manufacturer's mailing list and I am bombarded by catalogs, discount offers, merchandise, etc. But why change the process? I find another beauty, and sleep on the decision. Credit card out, laptop fired up, fingers crossed, and peeking with one eye to see the news. Nothing bad. Wow, really?

Order is up on the screen; credit card information being typed in as my phone rings. It is a dear friend, so I answer. "I had a little accident this morning on the way to the gym. I got knocked down off my bicycle by a woman making a left turn in her car."

Oh, dear Lord! I get it. God does not want me riding a bicycle! Perhaps He knows I would fall off it and smack my little head. I do not know for sure, but I also don't want to know that anyone else was hurt while He keeps trying to get me the message!

Each morning I ask for protection and guidance in my life. So why shouldn't I also ask to hear God's whisper?

To me that means being open to the possibility that the synchronicity in life is there for me. And on a personal level, it is demonstrating a willingness to accept the messages, no matter what form they take, and assimilating them into my life…into my day…into my decisions. Where it is easy to not make plans to travel to a dangerous part of the world, it is often more difficult to change normal, everyday activities or alter a decision one has already made.

May just be worth it though to listen to God's whispers.

3

Showers of Blessings

ಸಾಡ

Have you ever felt blessed? It is a wonderful, contented feeling in my experience. It is all about the feeling that comes along with saying the words: I am blessed. It is physical and emotional, and it is a good feeling. It is fantastic.

Words are powerful. They start wars, they sting, wound, and cause grief. But they also heal, warm, and can soothe and calm. Words bring out feelings, causing emotions to come to the surface even when those emotions have been hidden for years.

However, we take words for granted. We fling curse words to relieve tensions while driving and to our loved ones when we are angry. Tossing them into the air is one thing, but these declarations of hate will cut to the bone of those we care about. And the hurt might just be too deep to heal, even if soothing words of apology are offered. The indiscretion of saying something cruel may never truly be forgiven.

We need to think, to behave and to act with the knowledge of the power in our choice of words. But how do we start to do that?

Often our spirituality resides in a personal, special place within ourselves. When it does show itself, we understand all the wonder behind words such as love, spirit, blessing and the power of forgiveness.

We need to extend that knowledge and the experiences of those precious words into the rest of our lives:

...Into the part where we forget that cutting criticism is painful to the other person, even while we secretly pride ourselves at how spontaneously and cleverly, we cut them to the quick with our wit.

...Into the part of our lives where we correct a child harshly out of our own fear and ignore the truth that the child's life could possibly change direction because of our explosion of anger.

...Into the part of our lives where we sometimes need desperately to be right and dismiss being fair.

What would happen if we used any of these powerful tools for good? What if we considered what the person we are conversing with would love to hear? What if we changed the course of that adult's life by the words we carefully selected? We could shower a person, a friend, a loved one, with blessings.

So, I have to ask, what if this action changed our own lives by helping, guiding, and moving us forward into the person we always really wanted to become. Who we are is how we act, wouldn't you agree?

Choose words carefully. Very carefully. Consider the impact prior to throwing those words over to another person as you can never take those words back. Ever.

4

So, you want to see a miracle?

☙❧

On an afternoon with the sky just clearing from a week of storms, I arrived at a friend's home barely in time for us to leave for an appointment at 5 PM in another town. We were going to get a great deal on some furniture, and this was the last time available to see the wares. My friend went to confine her sweet, blind dog in the kitchen area of her home while we would be away, so the dog, Tobie, would not get hurt. But the dog was nowhere to be found in the home.

This was obviously perplexing since there was nowhere else for Tobie to be, and we had an appointment to go to. My friend tried to think back to the last time she saw Tobie and remembered that a neighbor had come to her front door about an hour prior, where they had chatted briefly. It was the only time a door to the outside was opened.

Could Tobie have slipped out without notice then? This was not a brave dog, especially since cataracts had taken her vision. And, Tobie would have had to walk down a short flight of steps to get to the front door. All this being the case, why had no one seen her leave?

Convinced that Tobie had been a masterful escape artist, and with the home situated on a steep hill, we decided to each take a car and scour the neighborhood. Time was pressing on that appointment we had, but we assumed Tobie could not be very far. After all, she couldn't see!

We cruised up and down the hills, shouting "TOBIE!!!!" for almost an hour when panic started to set in. We each asked every person we encountered if they had seen a little, white dog, or if they did see one to please call.

We had no idea how this could even be happening? How could this little dog get out of the house, let alone find her way anywhere? Tobie had not been out in front of her own home for a couple years. Calls to each other from our separate vehicles just heightened the already frightened atmosphere. And there was still no sign of little Tobie.

The sun was now setting; a good two hours had passed. No one would be buying furniture today. The storms that had pummeled the area for several days were now rolling back in with a sturdy breeze starting to kick up. Tobie, where could you be?

The little, blind Bichon was lost and alone in a coming storm. God, please help us find her!

Suddenly my friend is flagged down by a neighbor about seventy-five yards up the hill and across the street from where she lived. She's told there a small white dog behind the house up there.

This house has a very steep backyard facing a county park thick with trees. The house has a waist-high picket fence around the huge (practically vertical) backyard, and Tobie is outside that perimeter.

The steep hill and the mud from the storms made what might have been a simple rescue treacherous. It is also the kind of picket fence with slats very close together, and on both sides of the rail, so it wasn't possible to get the pup through the fence; or over it either as its just high enough not to be able to reach over and grab her.

Nearly everyone from the surrounding homes has now

gathered in the backyard of the pleasant young couple, who owned the property. It was quite the occasion with ideas pouring out of how to accomplish this task with a sightless, frightened dog, a steep hill, and lots of mud at center stage.

Another hour has now gone by. What would have been bedtime for the homeowners three-year-old has come and gone. The little girl, tired and half asleep, desperately wants to stay where all the excitement is happening. Besides, she is fascinated with the doggie.

All the efforts and generosity have paid off, a little possible trespassing aside, and one of the neighbors using a perfectly sized ladder and a lot of neighborly strength, pulls Tobie up and over the fence. Muddy Tobie is safe in my friend's arms. Everyone cheered! But suddenly a huge crash silenced the crowd.

Out in front of the very house where Tobie's escapades had come to an end, a huge tree, whose roots had given way due to the week's storms, had toppled onto the front corner of the home! The corner was crushed; the window shattered.

The bedroom that was in the front corner of that house belonged to the little three-year-old who fought sleep to see the doggie freed. Who, without Tobie's travels ending in her backyard, would have been put to bed in that collapsed room an hour or so earlier.

We have the choice to view this event any way we like. We can view it as a miracle...or as good fortune...or as luck.

You choose.

5

Guardianship

Are we responsible for our souls? Have they been put into our care while we travel as humans on this Earth? How can any act, any choice, influence our soul?

We may argue that nothing can change the fact that our souls will live on eternally, and I agree. However, I wonder if we can make choices which might alter the journey our souls take?

Do we decide on the course of our lives...or do we choose?

I like to think that prior to being born each soul meets with God, and He asks us to be challenged by certain things in this life we will have on Earth. It is our decision, and many will say, "Yes, Lord! I will do it for YOU!!" Of course, I also think that once we get down here and go through some of these experiences, we may ask ourselves, "What was I thinking???"

Circumstances are different for each of us as we come into the world. Gender, race, location, poverty, riches...the list goes on and on. Ultimately though, it is our choice how we live our lives and how we see life. Consider the possibilities if we each realized how powerful choice really is...

What will you choose?

I choose to live my life in the full expression of God's love.

I choose to surrender to God's timing of my life's events, knowing that everything that happens is for my protection and my guidance.

I choose to accept my life's purpose as a gift from God.

I choose to be a channel through which others can feel God's love.

I choose to surround myself with loving people who have an awareness of the loving God.

I choose to accept my humanness and the humanness of others.

I choose to remember that I am held firmly in the hands of God.

I choose to be true to myself.

I choose love.

6

The Thanksgiving Table

❧☙

Many of us intend to be thankful come Thanksgiving later this week. This is essentially a requirement, as most Thanksgiving tables will have us declaring what we are thankful for one-by-one. Being thankful for a meal or a day is easy. But what if our intention is to be thankful all the time? Could we pull that off?

Just about all spiritual writings about intention are about how important it is to have an intention for each of our actions, even for our lives. We are told it is a powerful, if not one of the most powerful forces under our control. What we claim our intentions are, however, is not always the persona that shows up!

Let us look at a family Thanksgiving:

Person #1: Is hosting Thanksgiving in his/her own home. This person just knows that everyone will want the same things for this day as they do. They also believe that each participant will do anything asked to make this family holiday a success. Not because this is how this family ordinarily behaves, but because it is a holiday and the family has not been together in a while. It is, therefore, important that this be a family only occasion.

Intention: Bring the family together for a lovely, congenial day together: preparing and cooking the dinner together, catching up on everyone's lives and activities, then culminating in a fantastic homemade dinner.

Person #2: Part of the same family as Person #1, however no longer living at home. Trying to spread his/her own wings, this person feels obligated (read: 'guilted' by Person #1) to participate in Thanksgiving with the family. Person #2 assumes, but never mentions that he/she plans to get some extra sleep, get up just in time to sit down to dinner, then exit the premises as soon as dinner is over.
Intention: Only see the family at dinner, then leave to visit with local friends.

Person #3: Part of the same family as Persons #1 and #2, currently living in the home of Person #1. Feels forced to stay home for Thanksgiving and would prefer to spend the day with Person #4, whom he/she is in a relationship with. It has been obvious since the relationship began, that the family is not very fond of Person #4. Person #3 has invited (required) Person #4 to come to dinner despite knowing Person #1 wants/expects a family only dinner.
Intention: Resentfully participate in the following manner...Be out of the house until the required dinner hour, bring Person #4 home without prior notice to Person #1, eat dinner, and then leave the house ASAP.

Person #4: See above. Would rather be anyplace else as he/she knows that Person #3's family is not supportive of the relationship. Carries at least a hint of resentment even before being told on the way to dinner that this is supposed to be family only.
Intention: Support Person #3, no matter what!

Have you ever heard of clashing intentions? I think this family has. Can you imagine this house during the hectic hours of dinner preparation, let alone the awkward attempts at conversation through dinner?

The real reasons for a person's actions are not always obvious and may prove quite the mystery. True intentions find their way out however, as they may come from age old resentments, hurts, or sorrows, and often these deeper feelings will not be denied. Certain gatherings, often the holidays, are when the past just loves to make an appearance!

We could agree that Person #1 shows good intentions. We could ask ourselves if they are realistic though, knowing the family dynamic here. But it is obviously what Person #1's goals are for the day. Much will depend on the others.

Why? Because one's good and even heartfelt intentions can backfire. It has happened to each of us at one time or another. When good intentions are met with extreme resistance and anger, everyone ends up hurt. More than likely the other person was offended by an offer and reacted defensively. Good intentions can fall far short of success when they are not accepted in the same spirit as they are offered.

When we set our intentions, we need to do it clearly, as these objectives are what affect our actions and interactions. More than that, we need to know ourselves, and align our intentions with our true selves. All this, with the understanding and compassion that everyone around us has their own intentions as well. It would have helped this family to vocalize what they really wanted and expected for that day.

With more and more practice, we can have peaceful gatherings, and joyful interactions. And we just might be more thankful all the time.

Happy Thanksgiving!

7

Joy

J oy is a wonderful word that is not used often enough. It is used in songs, particularly this time of year, but how often do we really use this word to describe something about ourselves or our feelings?

Joy is a powerful word expressing intense happiness and great delight. Elation. It is an emotional word of great pleasure. We, as a people, have trouble admitting to being happy. Feeling actual joy must seem a great stretch.

We need more joy in our lives!

Let us start now. Think of simple things that put a smile on your face. Find something that always brings that smile…

For me it is laundry. The very sound of a washing machine or dryer gives me the biggest smile. And yes, it truly brings me joy. Okay, go ahead and laugh, but here is why. I lived in apartments for many, many years…too many. Older buildings with many tenants sharing one washer and one dryer for ever increasing amounts of coinage.

I would have to gather my one load…or try for two… and carry that full load…trust me, a partial load wasn't worth the effort…as well as the detergent, softener, dryer sheet, and appropriate coinage, and my keys on quite the trek to the laundry facilities. I would load up, then exit the door of my apartment, walk down the hall, and call for the elevator. Free a hand to open the elevator door, press the right button, and go down to the first floor. There to exit the elevator, open the front door of the building, walk a few feet, use a separate key to open the door to the laundry area, then walk into that hallway, down a few stairs, and then use yet another key to open the laundry door. All that to find that someone was already there using the machine. Though there was pad and paper for tenants to note who was using the machine and when they would be done, it was not a habit most adopted.

Imagine the choices now. To carry the load, detergent, softener, dryer sheet, and coinage back out the door, down the hall, up the steps, out the other door, use keys to the open the front door of the building, call the elevator, walk down the hall, more keys for the apartment door, and then try to figure out when it would be possible for me to try this again. Or leave my items behind in the laundry room and try to time this adventure correctly. These experiences are the main reason I accumulated too many towels, bed linens, and too much underwear over the years.

The younger people in the building would do laundry very late into the night, and the older folks would have those machines going pre-5 AM. And two loads in a row was just a fantasy.

Now, in a home to call my own, with a laundry room no less, I can throw a load, of any size I might add, into the washer at any time of day or night. And yes, the sounds of that washer bring a sense of nothing less than joy to my little heart.

I also love to grow tomatoes. Every spring I tend lovingly to my little plants that miraculously produce juicy, edible tomatoes every single time. I even take pictures of them, and occasionally include them with Christmas cards. Yes, pure joy to be part of the creative, miraculous process of gardening and growing something edible.

And then there is Christmas…the miracle and promise that each December brings. You guessed it, joy to my heart.

I encourage you to find the joys in your life. They can be simple or extravagant. No rules apply here but to rediscover that there is joy in your life and to celebrate it. Once you recognize what brings you joy, remember what it is, and call it up again when you need a boost.

Celebrate also the great joy that Christmas brings. My wish for you this Christmas is that each of you, your families, and all your friends enjoy the blessings that this beautiful season offers. Feel the love that relationship offers. Open your mind and heart to possibility. Forgive and move forward with the hope of peace for all.

Express freely what is in your heart, whether it be a Merry Christmas, Happy Chanukah, or Happy Kwanzaa…. and when offered any of the above salutations, just say thank you!

May you be blessed.

8

Why Gardening?

❧☙

I grew up with a garden in my backyard. Though it was my grandparents who tended to it, I liked to check on how things were going. For example, I would pull up the carrots to see if they were ready yet to eat, and when they were still too small, would shove them back into the earth to grow more. That baby vegetable movement could have been all mine.

What I learned from watching my grandparents nurture the garden every season throughout the years is that most every day there was something to be accomplished in the garden. There were blossoms that graced our table from spring through fall. But their plants still needed to be tended to the rest of the year if they were to come back year after year. The fruits and vegetables that we harvested in late summer required tender loving care through late autumn and winter, as did the earth they grew in.

The way I see it, having a garden is the ultimate act of faith and love. Look at all the lessons gardening can teach us:

1. How to be optimistic;

2. How to have faith; and,
3. How to love.

Do you see how gardening is optimistic? Planting a seed in the ground, one expects that somewhere down the road, a plant will emerge. Isn't that pure optimism? The act is filled with hope. Isn't that faith? And a garden takes commitment, loyalty, and devotion. Isn't that love?

No one plants a garden not expecting success. Dreams of flowers or food fill the minds and hearts of many a first-time gardener. They start with beautiful optimistic visions of overflowing vases and cornucopias of abundance. So goes the soul garden when devotion is taken to heart.

Faith must be kept alive in the garden, for storms and pestilence will come. But hope will remain for a gardener with confidence.... for what good is faith if it is not tested?

Love. A garden requires what I call active love. Consider the act of being in love. Will that love flourish if no effort is put forth? One must love the garden in order to tend to it and nurture it throughout the seasons.

Gardens are often planted without knowing all that goes into the tending and nurturing required to keep them up. Many a garden has gone fallow without proper care. This was not necessarily the gardener's intention. That precious commodity called time, just gets filled with other demands.

We could say that gardening takes practice. We do not always get it right the first time. But with repetition and training, we get better at it.

As with gardening, we believe in certain things...we have faith in certain things. But often we lock them away in our hearts. We do not always practice them, tend to them, nurture them, or help them grow strong with roots that even when challenged will never yield.

This is what soul gardening can assist with. It can help us practice what we already believe and bring it out into the light of day.

In hindsight, what did I learn from my experience with carrots at an early age? That growth and maturity happen in God's time...not mine.

9

Hokey Pokey

☙❧

Ever hear of the Hokey Pokey? We used to sing it as kids. Everyone got in a big circle, and the lyrics were easy. We would do the Hokey Pokey and turn ourselves around. It didn't mean anything, it was just a fun way to get up, sing, and get everyone laughing.

The origins of the Hokey Pokey are uncertain. Whatever its beginnings, singing it was always lots of fun. But when I think of the Hokey Pokey, I think it represents a change of one's mind, a flip flop if you will. I believe we play Hokey Pokey with parts of our lives. In fact, I think it is how we treat our spirituality much of the time.

We put ourselves in when we celebrate our faith on holidays. We take ourselves out when we ignore our faith on other days. We put our hearts in when illness or other emotional storms strike. Then we pull ourselves out when the winds of change pass over and the pain recedes.

We do the Hokey Pokey, shaking up our thoughts and beliefs, taking them out in public when we dare, or hiding them when we are able. We turn ourselves around so often, we are not sure what we believe.

Life is not easy. Time is way too precious a commodity, especially these days. It is a difficult task just to get the chores done around the house, let alone dedicate time to the other things we need to do, or want to do, some we long to do.

My grandmother used to talk about Sunday Christians. She would tell me that the devil went to church every Sunday, because he already had the ones who stayed home. Grandma lived during a period when all the relatives shared the same faith, and stores were closed on Sundays. Television stations went off the air every night. Can we even believe that was the way it was? Back then, not everyone even had a TV.

Look at us now. Today's global marketplace and social media have transformed our world. Rather than go to church for a Bible lesson, the service comes to us on cable and Internet.

Yet one thing remains the same for many of us, and that is our desire to keep that channel open to our Creator.

A way to do that happened to me in a most unusual way. By way of friends, I was introduced to spiritual woman who, I felt, was rude and insulting to me. She told me I needed to read a certain book.[1] Some first meeting. I was wearing my pride that day and expected to hear that I was on the right path and had come so far. I was disappointed and my feelings were hurt.

Not sure why I would believe someone I had just met, unless she had told me what I wanted to hear! But that certainly was not the case. For some reason I bought and read that book, even though I was still hurt.

But, I knew exactly what the author's intention was. He was telling us to realize that every moment of our lives is being shared with God. Every breath, every action is in the company of God, and therefore, holy. And I liked that concept. So, I try to find ways to keep this idea in my consciousness.

Just like changing any habit, I would have to remind myself a lot. Just saying to myself, "This moment is holy" did not do a thing for me, as it had no real impact on me. So, I came up with an idea of how I could share my inspiration, without shouting on a street corner professing my faith. I decided to ask God to bless people. Quietly, and in my own way. Now we all need, and probably would be very happy to receive a blessing, but the truth is, I started out with people I felt could really use a blessing.

Yes, I do have to admit, it started with a person who had a limp or was using a cane. Maybe they were in a wheelchair, or it was the person pushing the wheelchair who got the blessing. Just a quick, and usually silent, "God bless you!" From the car, in a stadium, walking down the street. I got in the habit of doing it. I was bringing God to myself, and at the same time I was sharing Him. My reach expanded to the mom trying to handle wild children... or any children, to the driver with road rage, and even to an entire hospital if I happen to be driving past. Then it became every time I heard a siren, pass a car accident, or sometimes for no apparent reason. It was a gesture at first, an opportunity for me to remind myself of my spirituality. Now it is as earnest and profound as I can make it. It makes me happy, and I know that the blessings will hit their desired target.

I learned that every moment truly is holy. And I have shared that book multiple times.

I read a story once many years ago, where a woman in a car accident waiting for emergency crews to get to her, described seeing a ball of light rising into the sky from another car. The ball of light then came down and surrounded her. While she recovered in the hospital, the woman got a visit from a stranger who had witnessed the accident while driving and had come to see how she was doing. After lots of conversation, the hospitalized lady learned that her visitor had sent God's blessing to her at the accident scene...

We all need blessings. We all want to be blessed. So, Dear Lord, please Bless each person reading Soul Gardening right now.

10

Going Deep

☙❧

The dictionary's definitions for 'thankful' and 'grateful' are virtually interchangeable. The words are very different for me. Dictionaries cannot adequately put words to the emotions that mean so much to us. Thankfulness or gratefulness can be very emotionally charged, and words don't often suffice.

Normally, I don't use the words, 'I'm thankful' unless it is the beginning of a sentence at a Thanksgiving table. 'Thank you' to me is used predominantly as a simple acknowledgement of something someone else did, said, or gave. A gesture if you will. It is a socially acceptable way to display appreciation, lacking in feeling and intensity. It is a small kindness expressible to anyone at any time. "Thank you for holding the door open…"

However, when I use grateful, it is because I have a sincere feeling of the value of what I have been given. So, when I say 'I'm grateful' to someone for something, it is a much deeper, much more personal appreciation because I have internalized the gratitude.

In the past several years, a lot has been said, and books have been written, about being grateful. Gratitude journals are de rigueur in this enlightened age. I do not have one.

Please do not misunderstand. I believe gratitude is more than just fashionable. It is a necessary part of a healthy, normal life. But I also believe that making a list at the end of the day is simply that...a list.

A list is a list is a list. Make all the lists you want, shopping lists, honey do lists, gratitude lists. Do it every single day. And it will still be just a list unless you go deep. And when you do go deep, you will not need that list any longer.

Let's look at these lists for a moment. When you put items in your gratitude journal, do you feel them for more than the minute it takes to write them? Do they bring you joy as you write? Can they make you weep just by thinking of them? Do you feel the love that is such an integral part of that gratitude?

Going deep means that you touch the deepest part of your emotional being. We may not always like it, but we are emotional beings. God has given us a plethora of emotions as part of our human make up. We don't seem to be very fond of many of those emotions. The happy, joyous, pleasant ones are a hit. Not so much the others.

We need to learn to be grateful from deep within our hearts. Doing this will not only make gratitude work for us, but it will also have some incredible side effects.

If I truly believe that I am protected and guided, (a theme here with Soul Gardening), then I will find the things that show me exactly that.

Prior to asking for and I believe receiving that protection and guidance, I have had experiences where I have forgotten my credit cards at home and was forced to return there before I could continue my journey. I would get so angry at myself. I would swear and slam doors, and just become totally stressed out that my plans had taken an unpleasant turn.

Let's say traffic on any given day was not cooperating, and I was going to be late for an appointment. Frustrated? Oh yeah. Ticked off? You bet.

Enter the possibility of Gratitude Attitude. The mindset where you can live your gratitude.

I have learned, and now choose to know that yes, I am protected and guided every single day. In that choosing, I can find peace and even comfort in forgetting something at home that requires a stop back there. I can say okay to a traffic jam. Why? Because God doesn't want me on the road quite yet, or He's holding me tight in a certain spot. He is keeping me safe on my journey which is exactly what I asked Him to do!

So, the other day, I had an appointment in a city two hours away. And when I stopped at a station for gas, and the card reader didn't work. I was not happy to get back into the car and drive to the next station. There the card reader worked, but the pump itself didn't work. So off I went to the third pump, which only provided about six ounces of gas at each click of the handle. The frustrated feeling started to rise because I did not leave enough time for all this foolishness. But I then looked upwards and said, "I get it! You don't want me on the highway just yet." So, I stood there, and patiently pumped the gas six ounces at a time until my tank was full. I also said, "I'm so grateful You are watching out for me!"

The side effects I mentioned? Choosing a Gratitude Attitude can not only bring peace and comfort knowing we are taken care of, but it can also eliminate the stress, anger, and frustration of a situation where we are not in control.

It has changed my life going deep with the emotion of heartfelt appreciation. It has created a way for me to feel the love of being protected and cared for by my loving God.

11

Amen

ꙮ

Now a fond memory for me is any holiday dinner while my maternal grandparents were still alive. The mornings were filled with much preparation. The peeling of the potatoes, carrots and other veggies along with the ouchies when the peeler nicked a piece of skin. The slicing and the dicing began for the stuffing, for packaged dressing was not even a glimmer in some entrepreneur's eye yet. Then the sautéing, the soaking of the bread, and finally the creation of a yummy stuffing for an enormous bird that barely fit into the oven.

Then the hours of beautiful rich smells that filled the house along with the arriving family that warmed the house into a home. A truly fabulous meal was just hours away. The family caught up with each other on news and gossip while we waited for the feast. There was always a temptation to snack on something, but no one did as we could hardly wait to dine on all of our favorites that always showed up on grandma's table.

And then the moment came when the culinary magic was finally unveiled and elegantly plated. One by one the serving dishes were carried in procession from the kitchen to the formal dining room and placed gently on the large table which had been carefully padded and covered with a hand embroidered tablecloth, napkins, shiny glassware, and flowers. The good silver too. The dining room table was now laden with so many plates of food that some must go atop the credenza on the side of the room.

We then gathered happily and hopefully around the amazing presentation; spirits high in anticipation. And, of course, there must be grace, the giving of thanks. Not the daily "Lord bless this food" kind of grace. It must be the kind that truly celebrates the occasion of all of us being together. Parents, children, children's children, cousins together after semesters away, and the occasional new baby attending his first family tradition.

We bow our heads, and there she blows. My dear Aunt Emma bestows us with a beautiful oratory of a grace worthy of this celebration. "Dear Heavenly Father" it usually began...

And the delightful smells and sheer hunger betray my young heart, and while all heads are bowed with eyes closed in gracious silence, I am sneaking something off the turkey platter. Auntie just keeps going, God bless her, and I can nab some irresistible stuffing to satisfy these day long cravings. I have minutes to steal and take advantage of every taste I desire.

By the Amen, I am lucky to have had quite a few amuse-bouches. And you know, a stolen bite tastes exquisitely better!

Here is the thing, what good is a prayer if one is just reciting words, or standing there waiting for it to be over? I think it must mean something. What is the point of reciting any of the prayers we learned as kids? Does that in any way make us more grateful or appreciative?

It doesn't unless, you guessed it, unless we mean the words. We must do more than just listen to what is being said or recite what we have a million times. We are obligated to pay attention. We need to be in the present moment, and it is essential to feel the words. We must take the words in as if they are our own.

My precious grandfather, even in his 70's and 80's when I knew him, taught me more about prayer than anyone who ever spoke to me about it. Grandpa had some bad knees but every single morning and every evening without fail, that lovely man would get down on his knees in front of a dining room chair and he prayed. He would stay maybe twenty minutes or so, then get up and get on with his day, or his night.

This daily action was not talked about; no one ever made mention of it. It was simply a demonstration of his faith. It was public in a family sense as that dining room chair was in a room right in the middle of the house. And his actions left an incredible impression on me.

I used to pray before bed as a child. Always for things I wanted, and then a quick please bless my family. But as I grew realized that praying for 'things' is not what prayer is about. So, I sought new ways to be grateful for all I have and all the gifts I have been given from above. I explored other prayers to see if they resonated with me. I particularly like the prayer of Jabez.

Gratefulness and appreciation have expanded from nightly prayer right into my days, and lately I'm thinking of every day as a prayer. It is my personal communication with my Creator, my Counselor, and my Friend. As I think of it in this way, I become even more grateful for my life, my friends, and my family. There are days in which I see His gifts in everything I see and do.

That wonderful man, my grandfather, in his quiet and unassuming ways, demonstrated for me, a personal relationship with Him that I cherish now myself. And to that I gratefully say, amen.

12

Chaos

෨ඣ

We live in a chaotic world; time seeming to move faster every day. We chase after the technological advances we love – fancy phones, TVs, virtual reality, and the rest. I say 'chase' as no matter when I buy something new, the very next week, it is being replaced by something that does even more. We have commitments that promise our lives away, and often jobs that are extremely demanding.

The chaos touches every single part of our lives. Even email is not fast enough anymore, so now we must text each other. We don't want to get together with friends and family because it is just too much trouble. Besides we know how they all are. We did just get an instant message or saw a Facebook post the other day. Too much trouble to talk on the phone too. Just text and include an emoticon. Pictures are worth a thousand words, right?

Guess we are all just trying to control the commotion that's in our faces every moment. Let's face it, at the end of the day we always think there is something we still must do, forgot to do, or need to do.

What most of us are not realizing is these technological marvels, these activities that everyone has too many of, the pressure to keep up and keep moving, these are just giving us excuses for every other commitment we might normally have. Too little time. Too little energy.

This atmosphere may have ruined our true connections to those who are important to us, and that doesn't just mean friends and family. We are missing out on our very lives. And what's worse? The chaos has become the white noise that we do not know how to live without.

When we lose ourselves, we lose our connection to who we truly are: Spiritual beings. We end up in a state of spiritual complacency. After all, we know what we believe, and just tuck it inside for safe keeping. It is safe there, isn't it?

In the search for something more, or in realizing we have lost ourselves; we often hear that we should meditate or pray. Yes indeed, just shut off that chaos in an instant. We are supposed to go within and get our overly active minds to shut up. Perhaps we can contemplate our navels or maybe we will just fall asleep. The bedlam in our lives does have a way to keep us awake, and often we just need some sleep. More easily said than done. And yet if one can put on some music, read a little, lounge in a hot bath, it surely does feel good.

My experience is that the moment that little piece of goodness, that quietness ends, I am right back in the madness. Why? Because it's just one more item on the 'to do' list. Yeah, I got it done. So what?

I had to start looking at the chaos differently. I imagined that I am the Earth, and the chaos is the space debris orbiting around me in the atmosphere. Visualizing that I can separate myself from the space junk.... the half million plus pieces of satellite parts, rockets, and trash flying around. The space junk, also known as my responsibilities, appointments, work and activities, and other demands put on me largely by me.

What I did was that rather than make my meditation or prayer just another item on the proverbial 'to do' list, I added it to the chaos. Now hear me out. I add it to the chaos, so I have to deal with it every single day. But I added it as something I 'want' to do...not as something I 'have' to do. When we want to deal with something every day, we bring it into the present moment. This is a very good thing.

First, we decide what we would like to add to our current pandemonium. We may make the choice to bring God into or back into our lives. How will we do that? Will we start by each morning saying, "Thank You for this beautiful day?" Perhaps we will say grace with our meals? Will we say a "Bless you" when seeing someone in need? Start with something that doesn't require the time and energy that we have so little of. Just a small addition that will bring our attention to God.

It is very important to be gentle with yourself, as it may take a little time for this new routine to establish itself. Ponder on it. If it is something you truly want in your life, it will happen.

Once this is a habit, and when it makes you feel better for doing it, add something else. Pretty soon you will find the miracle in adding such things to your chaos. You will find that your actions have actually created a tunnel through the commotion and disarray, and out into that beautiful open Universe where God also resides, and you can look down on the chaos and the Earth (your life), with a perspective unlike one you have ever known. You have become an observer rather than a participant in the chaos.

You have made a new connection to the Source. You will eventually find yourself at peace with the chaos that surrounds you, while enjoying your Creator with a different and more beautiful perspective.

13

Spring

ಬ ಡ

Spring is magical. It is like there is something special in the air: crisp, fresh and filled with promise and anticipation. I love the feeling of spring fever as it makes me long for fresh flowers in the house, and something growing outside. Cannot wait to make that first trip to the nursery to see what treasures they have already started for me in the greenhouse. Its springtime folks, and time to get our hands dirty.

Life awakens in springtime. We are surrounded by the splendor of God's creations. We take a deeper breath as the reawakening of Nature happens all around us. It is time to nurture what has been ignored.

Garden clean up starts as the earth warms. The planet increasingly tilting its axis toward the sun, allowing daylight to provide us those longer days we all love. It won't be long before the glorious sunshine stretches late into our evening hours. Oh yes. The earth has rested and is ready to put forth every ounce of energy to become the very best environment for the bulbs and seeds that will look to the soil for support, structure, and nutrients.

Time to plan the Soul Garden as well, whose growing environment is how well we live our lives. Well, in the sense of living true to our beliefs and values, and how we carry those values into the world. Well, in where we focus our energy, and how we support and distribute that energy into our day-to-day lives.

We have choices to make every day that will affect our Soul Garden. We display our beliefs and values in the way we behave in the world. Do we live our beliefs? Or put them aside for some immediate gratification? Do we support our values? Or yield to someone else's idea of what is acceptable?

So, what is it that we shall plant this glorious season? Shall we start small with perhaps a container garden, and just try to foster growth one seedling at a time? Perhaps we decide that our lives really need a change of direction, and plant all the important values we have always admired and wanted to display?

One may find that there are already a few plants in the Soul Garden. Perhaps some seeds of indulgence have sprouted? Or seeds of greed have taken root? There's a good chance we will want to replace those shrubs with some seeds of inspiration, motivation, or even intention.

Shall we start with the seeds of compassion? The bulbs of forgiveness? Perhaps some 'old roots' of generosity and gratitude are still deeply embedded, and can be encouraged to sprout again? If we choose to nurture some 'old roots', we must remember to treat them as tenderly as the buds of the new seeds and bulbs.

And always remember to have patience. The environment for growth must be strong enough to hold and support our seedlings, yet soft enough to allow for the roots to take hold. We must enrich the environment with persistence and tolerance. And never forget, active love. What better gift to give our Soul Garden than daily attention?

As these plants grow, know that we will be cultivating joy, for joy is not a seed, but much like a harvest that is the result of encouragement and nurturing.

So, are you still wondering why you would take the time to plant and nurture a Soul Garden? Because we reap what we sow!

14

This Singular Journey

෪ ཚ

We are on a journey. A singular journey on the road less traveled. The destination is set, but the means of travel and the stops along the way will be quite unique. Ours is a journey of the heart that, at times, we will long to share with others. This will not always be easy, for you see, this trip must be taken alone. And in the grand scheme of things, it is understandable that it must be this way. For this is a journey into relationship with God.

Like most solo treks, it is important to have a good idea of our intentions. Our destination is to understand as much as possible about the Source of all things. In the process of that learning, we must also be willing to share ourselves on a new and deeper level. We can each travel at our own pace, and jog off in a new direction when something catches our eye. Who knows what side trips will pop up out of nowhere, or who we may meet on this path?

There are no rules here, but we may want to employ some of the same tactics we use for travel. We will want to be flexible and take plenty of side trips, for example, like visiting places of worship of all faiths. Call ahead. The faithful can be very welcoming.

Remember to ask the 'locals' for information only they can provide about their faith. Keep an open mind, and don't judge. This is the expedition of a lifetime, and as the adventures continue, memories will be made that will last forever. We should be curious and of course, be respectful. Patience will go far. The traditions of others can explode our own original concepts of how to worship, how to love God, and how to surrender.

All relationships are a process. They take time, energy, and attention. This new relationship has the possibility to bring us closer to finding peace in our lives. We will be shown things we never thought we would feel or see. Our understanding of the very nature of God will help us to develop a connection only a few will ever have.

This remarkable relationship can be so close that we will long to communicate almost constantly. Every day can become a prayer. We will yearn to show Him how much we care daily. Our clearer priorities will shift our thoughts and actions, and at the same time create a desire to strive to learn more and more about God.

Our openness will hit new strides, and our compassion and desire to offer forgiveness will skyrocket. And yes, relationships are both give and take. So, what would you like from the Lord? Would you like to see God's miracles or hear His whispers? Ask, and ye shall receive. We will start to wish that all our friends and family could have similar experiences, and perhaps they will in their own time.

We will feel loved, and blessed, as well as discover a sense of comfort because we have entered into relationship with a God who loves us more than we can ever return. He who just wants us to get to know Him and ask Him into our lives. The journey starts with a short stroll, or as the hymn goes, "Just a Closer Walk with Thee."[2]

15

Hallelujah!

ଈଓ

Time for more celebration as Passover and Easter are upon us. I grew up coloring too many Easter eggs. What does one do with literally dozens of hard-boiled eggs? Russell Stover solid chocolate bunnies, and always a new Easter outfit were a part of our annual celebration. And then there was that one commemorative picture out in the backyard. Those were the days my friends. And those chocolate bunnies are still a part of my celebration.

Passover and Easter are 'movable feasts.' Though they are annual celebrations, they don't fall on the same days each year. The days vary based on the sun and the moon, and if you want to get into the details, the Gregorian and Hebrew liturgical calendars.

One of the things I most enjoy, besides chocolate bunnies, is finding commonalities that I didn't know existed. Recently I am discovering links between the Old and New Testaments that are mind-blowing. These two holidays, for example, are linked in many ways, besides both happening in the spring. For example, the words for Passover and Easter come from the same root words.

Passover celebrates God sparing His people from slavery in Egypt. Think for a moment about the Jewish sacrificial

Passover Lamb, and the reality that Christian's call Jesus the Lamb of God.

Then reflect on the symbolism of the last supper. At His last Passover with the disciples, Jesus used bread and wine to represent His body and blood. Offering forgiveness, or the 'passing over' of our sins.

Jesus's death took place during the daylight hours following Passover, which makes it the same day as Passover. A day being sunset to sunset. So, Jesus was sacrificed on Passover. Christians believe that Christ is the Passover Lamb.

Moving one holiday further out on the Jewish calendar, is the seven-day Feast of Unleavened Bread, which immediately follows Passover. The feast celebrates the Israelites escaping Egyptian slavery so quickly, that they could not leaven their bread. It was during this same period that Jesus was raised from the dead. This resurrection symbolizing the releasing of us from our sin.

I love the parallels from Old and New Testaments written some four hundred years apart. And I love celebrating the true meaning of Easter, as it represents the purest joy in celebrating Jesus's divinity. That from great loss comes the promise of rebirth.

We say a lot of Hallelujahs in the spring. Hallelujah meaning 'God be praised' or 'Praise ye the Lord.' The difference depends on whether we use the Greek or Hebrew translation.

Amongst our Easter eggs, Passover Seder, and family gatherings, consider all the historical and religious occurrences that created these celebrations in the first place. Appreciate the hope and promise that the Passover blessings of grace, protection, and God's favor bring. For Christians, this is the most sacred Sunday of the year, where we rejoice in the commemoration of the resurrection of Jesus and His ascension to heaven.

Time will always be precious. Take some moments to be with your Creator. Fully recognize your ability to sow your faith in your life. Plant your renewed devotion into your days, and scatter your spiritual thoughts as you would seeds, into all your activities. May they blossom and bless you and yours in their thriving. My Easter wish is that we each learn to bask in Divine Presence.

16

God is Not One Religion

ಸಾರ

I inherited an open mind toward faith. When I grew up the question we kids asked each other was, "What are you?" That meant, what church do you go to? Everyone had an answer back then. I am sure it was the time and the place, as that would not be true today. And once the question was asked, the answer was forgotten because it wasn't a part of what made a kid a friend.

My family practiced different forms of Protestantism, but our friends came in all faiths and cultures. My maternal grandmother, as a part of her immigration to the United States in the early nineteen hundreds, found herself in a city where every couple blocks different cultures and religions thrived. While the men went off to work each day, the women gathered. They learned to speak various languages, learned about different cultures, shared food, participated in celebrations, etc. And the appreciation for all of this continued in my family through the generations.

It was a like a trip around the world to go to weddings, baptisms or Christmas dinners and Passover Seders with people who were dear to my family but practiced their own faith. Catholic, Greek Orthodox, Jewish, Methodist, Presbyterian, Assembly of God, and Baptists...all the same in that they were friends.

Many of these celebrations took place in different churches, and it was always enchanting to see what new ritual was introduced to my life experiences. Speaking in tongues, golden interiors, statues, the smoke of burning incense, the chanting of monks. This was captivating to me, and it continues to be.

Google how many religions there are in the world and it is estimated to be more than four thousand. Evidently my experience with religion is more limited than I previously hoped. Hard to imagine all that I am missing out on here.

That number alone helps me to understand why folks are more likely now to say they are 'spiritual' rather than 'religious.' The word religion has taken on a connotation in today's world, implying strict cultural systems, set beliefs, as well as specific world views and precise moral values. It all sounds rigid and demanding.

Aren't people more likely say life is hard enough without more demands and rules? Religion has taken on a public aspect now, which makes spirituality feel more personal and compassionate.

There are religions with multiple gods, and many with none. Several religions have one God, while some say that the one God is really three. The differences fascinate me, and I am curious about when each came into being, and what was going on in the world when that happened.

I love the pomp and circumstance of Catholicism. I have shed tears at the mere sight of Michelangelo's Pieta, and been known to wrap my arms around a pillar in Paris's Notre-Dame. I admire that Jewish temples are used as places of study and as community centers. And I have to say that the Blue Mosque in Istanbul, is one of the most spiritual places I have ever encountered in my lifetime. One must remove their shoes prior to entering the beautiful structure, and the feeling inside was one of intense sacredness. Having the opportunity to celebrate with and receive blessings from Buddhist monks has been as holy an experience as I have ever had.

These all touch my heart in a way I find hard to describe because the experience is so personal. The people I have met were all lovely and tremendously willing to share their beliefs and celebrations.

To experience life through the different rituals means that each connection and every shared moment becomes a part of who I am, a part of my celebration of my love of God. Not that I can't have a memory made in my own backyard, or standing in Yosemite or Zion National Park, but I try to take in these moments and burn them into my experiential memory. Moments I can recall at any time and be there once again. The feelings come back so easily; it is like they were yesterday.

This is my journey, and I love it. What other religious practices bring me is an enhancement to my soul garden. It enriches my existence, develops my appreciation, and heightens my gratitude. Whatever my love for God is, I find it amplified even as I delight in Buddhist traditions that omit Him. For my God wants me to be happy and joyful, so I bring Him along as I celebrate with others. It all gives meaning to my life.

Therefore, no matter what building you may pray in, no matter the religion you practice, or that you say you are recovering from, may you find peace and joy in it, and open your heart to the thousands of other possibilities.

17

Rainbow Bridges and Doggie Doors

☙ ❦

The fact that there is serious debate about whether pets go to heaven does not matter to me. Theologians have argued, and even the Pope joined the discussion recently. My heart admired Pope Francis for speaking out, and declaring that animals will join humans in the kingdom of heaven. I am feeling particularly grateful for that reassurance now that I have had to put my little dog Tucker to sleep. He was only seven years old but filled my life with wonder and joy every single day with his happiness and sweet personality.

    I wish I could live by Tucker's example. He started every day with a smile and a stretch. The smell of his food created excited barking and spinning in circles, which was supposed to get me to move faster putting the food down on the floor. He napped daily, and always lowered his body slowly when laying down as if emulating a yoga master. At all times he rose into that slow stretch and was then raring to go…anywhere! And he just loved to ride in the car, and he so loved going to bed at night. He was asleep it seemed, as soon as he laid his head down.

It didn't matter where I wanted to go; he just wanted to come with me. His enthusiasm was contagious. This same enthusiasm often annoyed the cat, but then so did any other action or noise that disturbed her.

When one speaks of unconditional love, I swear they can only be speaking about God or a dog. Both forgive me no matter what and love me even when I screw up. I certainly could not ask for anything more.

With Tucker I was in communion with life, and the appreciation of such. He welcomed me home as if I had been gone an eternity and would sit with me no matter my mood. His eyes always looked at me lovingly. It was a responsibility I took very seriously to care for him and make the right choices on his behalf. Our connection was singular. Though I will have other dogs in my life, the time spent with Tucker will be unique.

This is the same kind of nurturing and caring that Soul Gardening is all about. The active kind of love that shows you are there for those you love. You nurtured and were unconditionally loved in return. You tended to their needs, and they tended to yours.

The Bible doesn't address the issue of pets as such. The possible exception is the poor man who had nothing save a ewe lamb. The Bible says the lamb shared his food, drank from his cup, and slept in his arms. It was like a daughter to him.

Using that as an example, and the fact that I know my God to be loving and generous, I look forward to being reunited with my little Tucker when my life is over. My fur children mean the world to me, and heaven just would not seem enough without the knowledge that they will be there with me. When I left Tucker's side, I kissed him, and told him I would see him in heaven. For those are my plans.

If you know the story of the Rainbow Bridge, you believe that pets go to a beautiful green meadow when they die. The pets romp and play in the perfect field while waiting for their humans to pass. Once reconnected, the pets and the owners will cross the bridge together, walk into heaven, and never be separated again.

Or perhaps you believe that God put a doggie door in the Pearly Gates? Either way, it is my choice to believe that will happen. If you have ever loved a pet, I believe you feel the same way. But I also think, maybe there is a reason that dog is God spelled backwards?

18

To Everything There is a Season

❧❦

Writing this book brings me the greatest joy, and I usually cannot wait to craft the next story until today. And perhaps that gives me something to write about? I lost my little dog, Tucker, a couple weeks ago. It was hard on all of us. Gracie, the cat, especially because she loved the little guy. The other dog, Dakota, and I are recuperating from the different activity level, but my brain is lost in not having something to focus on and care for with such intensity.

You see, once Tucker was diagnosed with lymphoma and kidney disease, and I was advised there was great success in treatments, I was on board with chasing a healing. So, for almost seven months of Tucker feeling well, and being his playful self, I was frantically intent on making him the miracle dog who was going to beat these diseases. Every pill, and there were many a day, every meal, was something to accomplish. All test results were logged into a spreadsheet to watch his progress, and every new medication was researched on the Internet. I was like a terrier in pursuit of a long life for my companion.

Long story short, when the time came, and Tucker was not having a happy life any longer, he went to the Rainbow Bridge. I cried, and cried, and expected a period of grieving. I knew I had done everything I could and had no guilt for putting him to sleep. But what I didn't realize at the time was how much hope died also.

Hope is a wonderful elixir. It is a big piece of love and life. We all have hopes and dreams, and they give us great reasons to actively pursue the good things we desire in life. Hope essentially equals joy. It is optimism and courage rolled into one.

So, when any hope is lost, we end up discovering some of those emotions we humans are not fond of, bubbling to the surface of our life. Right now, I find myself worrying about me and everything else, anxious about life in general, and, of course, not sleeping. That protective layer of confidence has been eroded by the loss, and ultimately the defeat of the hope and longing for Tucker to be healed, and for his life to continue.

But I know these feelings need time to pass. All emotions need to be honored because they are a part of our makeup as human beings. It is not easy, because all we want is for these particularly painful emotions to be over with as soon as possible. Yet in my experience if they are not felt, they linger and bury themselves inside me until I let them out... sometimes years later!

For now I try to find comfort in the things I believe I can trust, particularly "A time to weep, and a time to laugh; a time to mourn, and a time to dance; A time to cast away stones, and a time to gather stones together; a time to embrace, and a time to refrain from embracing; A time to get, and a time to lose; a time to keep, and a time to cast away." *(Ecclesiastes 3: 4-6 KJV)*

Time will heal. Music always helps me. Listen to the song, Turn! Turn! Turn! (To Everything There is a Season) by The Byrds. Released in 1965.

I put in the time and effort to forge the hope, now I must let the loss of it have its season as well. For "To everything there is a season unto Heaven…"

19

Maranatha Park and Broadway

~~~

One room cabins in this old Bible Camp hold sweet memories of childhood for me. A ginormous tabernacle held the faithful most every summer evening; its doors folded open not only to allow for a summer's breeze, but also for the glorious music to permeate the sparkling country air.

Maranatha Park was in Green Lane, Pennsylvania, a two-hour drive from home, and yet world's away. It was just like camping. Most cabins didn't have indoor plumbing or running water. Laundry was done on a washboard in a big tub. The wet clothes hung on rope strung between two trees. The distance often too great causing the wet clothes to land on the ground if not for the ingenious use of very tall 2x4's that propped up the middle of the rope.

Sounds horribly primitive, but it was a very special place for my grandparents to relax in the country and worship. As unsophisticated as it was, this campground had restorative powers over the participants.

The days were hot, and the afternoons brought on a laziness, moving the gentlemen to nap and the ladies to have tea in small cliques, their gossiping betraying their nightly prayers. We had radio, but no television, and the Internet hadn't yet been created. Handheld devices were still dreams of people not yet born. If one became antsy, you probably went for a walk down to the river, and if luck was on your side, a thunderstorm would rumble through, echoing thunder loud enough to scare the bravest soul.

The cabins weren't more than fifty feet apart. One walked over tree roots, and rocks between cabins to get to the tabernacle or the snack bar. A flashlight was necessary to get home after the evening services as there were no streetlights. But there weren't streets either, just dirt roads, and certainly no property lines or fences.

The tabernacle was filled to capacity at every service. Rousing sermons, and my favorite, plenty of singing. The presence of the Lord was felt strongly, and hands were raised in praise. It was all God, all the time, and the vibe was unadulterated love and joy. The music wafted past the cabins and into the fields to offer God's presence to all the surrounding countryside.

It seemed to me that the music was still in the air long after the services – it not only carried us all the way home, but also gave the impression of gently putting us to sleep.

So when my grandparents took their trips to Heaven, we didn't keep Green Lane. The mystique the cabin once held was lost on the next generation, and I had hit teenage by then and found Broadway was only a bus ride away. I fell in love with musicals, and almost tried to make that a career. Musicals were, and still are my absolute favorite way to spend a day or a night in New York City.

Put together someone who fell in love with religious music as a child, then quickly developed a love and appreciation for Broadway musicals, and what to you get? A church choir member for life.

Let me tell you something you already know deep inside of you. Music impacts our brains and arouses our emotions and feelings more powerfully than words. You know what I am talking about. Happy, sad, however we are feeling, we turn to music. Music has that special healing quality we need.

Sermons aren't always my favorite thing, but I sure can feel His love when I'm singing. Go on, get closer to your Creator by singing. What a perfect way to worship. At least it is my favorite way to love Him in this life.

20

Namaste

ఎఁలఁ

Learned any Sanskrit lately? Namaste is a great word to start with. It means I bow to the God within you. Just take that in for a second. I acknowledge that you are created by God, just as I am. My soul is acknowledging your soul.

And that incredible consideration, said with hands together as if in prayer and usually along with a slight bow, is the way many around the world begin a greeting, an introduction, a conversation, or a debate. Feels amazing to think about. Honoring someone we just met, and then proceeding from that point.

The obvious comes to mind. Imagining a world where prejudice and bias are rarely used nouns with definitions we must look up for their lack of use. It is like declaring, God created me, so you must be fabulous as well.

I must wonder if absorbing that consciousness into our own being would help us to find meaning in our lives. The true meaning of life has been debated since the beginning of time. Whether it is that we exist for the pleasure of God, or because He thought we would find and have happiness in the flesh, I don't know.

We seem to discover meaning in our lives when we

involve our hearts; when we nurture; when we love and are loved. Many find meaning in living their faith. Yet there are folks who think they just do not have time in their lives for that right now. What they are not realizing is that each one of us is living our beliefs every single day. Does that surprise you to hear?

Our behavior represents our deepest feelings, beliefs, fears, hopes, dreams. Everything. So, when we say we wish someone else was warmer, nicer, happier, or we wish we had more joy in our lives, the real meaning is that we need to alter our own personal belief system and our own personal values.

We claim we are not prejudiced, but we cross the street when a person of another race is walking towards us. We say we are charitable, but we don't offer assistance to someone down on their luck when we don't think they are doing enough to help themselves. We say we believe in loving our neighbors but trash them to other friends. We say we believe in God but are afraid to bring that up in conversation. Most of us learned the Golden Rule as kids, but how often do we follow it?

We are so afraid of each other, despite so many millions of people following the religious teachings of Buddha and Jesus Christ. For that matter kindness is at the core of each of most major religions. So why do we find it so easy to be unkind to one another?

We no longer honor life as being as precious as it is. At least not until a tragedy comes along, or some loved one is at the end of life. We honor individuals we trust and love, some that we respect at least until we judge them unworthy.

We have made ourselves judge and jury of everything and everyone. Perhaps if in our deepest selves we knew true happiness and felt real joy at our core, we could change the world. The outward expressions that would be produced from that happiness and joy would surely give us a great start.

Each of us has a different understanding of the world. Our varied experiences have created that diversity. And yet we all want to be loved and appreciated. We can start by loving and demonstrating it. Should that prove too difficult, we could start with showing some respect. This truly starts with us, and it starts at this very moment. So, let us begin our interactions with each other in a way that brings our hearts and minds into the agreement that we are all equally created by God.

Let us begin. Namaste!

21

The Plight of the Slightly Enlightened

፠ଊ

Anyone want to volunteer to be one of the 'slightly enlightened?' I will. Yes, that is just how I think of my life sometimes. Just trying to be a better person, and not always succeeding. I have done my fair share of reading, listening, participating in seminars, some by famous people, many from just 'Sam and Sally Spiritual.' Wonderful people, Sam and Sally.

The intention was always to learn more about God, myself, humanity, spirituality, and as it turns out, life here on Earth. Many of us assume we know all about the religion we grew up with as kids. We just decide we did not like a certain part of it, so we cut ourselves off from continuing to practice it without full knowledge of our faith's origins, beliefs, or current state of purpose. Some try to hang on to principles such as the Golden Rule, or some commandments, but many of us want something more than what we have. So, we decide to go outside of organized religion to seek meaning and purpose.

There is so much out there to assist. In the old days there was Est and Silva Mind Control. A Course in Miracles came along, as well as energy attunement workshops, soul fusion, crystal healing classes, shamanism, metaphysics, auric power, spiritual healing classes, Reiki seminars, books and movies from Shirley MacLaine, and on and on. There are religious studies as well that some of us take on, and no matter what is chosen, we still need acceptance and love to carry on successfully in our lives.

No matter what we have or have not done outside of day to day living life, I think we all would love to figure out what our life's purpose is, why we're here, and how to be happiest in the pursuit of it all. We often try to share this information with others and quickly learn who is into our pursuit of this type of knowledge, and who is not.

We will find at some point along this priceless journey that the outside information from books and workshops all starts to sound similar...much like a broken record. The information is invaluable as it is being heard, however once the book closes or the weekend is over, the implications and wonder fade into day-to-day routine. This occurs often enough, and one wonders, so what really is next?

Next is culpability. One of those big words that mean we have to do something with what we have, and what we have learned. It is where we practice what was preached, so we can absorb it into our consciousness. It is where we try out the methods, we have so enjoyed learning about.

Why do we have to do this? It is the way we learn, and it is called practice. Just like learning mathematics or even how to garden. Those times tables from the fourth grade were learned by saying them repeatedly.

Look at gardening. Can one learn to garden by buying a potted plant? Nope. We cannot start at the end. We cannot read a book or participate in a seminar and finish it, and then expect our entire life to suddenly change into what we just experienced.

So, practice it is. Keep in mind that practice is the hardest part of anything one wants to learn. Let us start with something relatively easy. For example, try out the concept that we are all equal in the sight of God. As you meet people or hear stories in the news, what is your reaction to their race, gender, appearance?

We cannot be afraid of reactions we are not completely proud of, as this is about learning our true beliefs and values. It is only by knowing what is down in our subconscious that we can bring about change. We must give ourselves permission to become introspective. This is a courageous gift to give oneself.

Catching those unwanted reactions as they occur is the first step toward change. Catch and throw out a new image. Pull a weed and plant a seed. Now that is Soul Garden talk. So, in recognizing a disparaging thought toward a person, change it to, for example, a "God bless you." Who couldn't use a blessing after all?

What we are doing is allowing ourselves to manifest kindness in the place of malice. Allow the feeling of love for a human being. Truth is, this is hard enough with people we love, let alone strangers. But it is all about the practice, repetition, and desire behind the action.

Okay, again. Yes, practice is all about the again…

Our first reaction to things can change from anger to compassion.

Who couldn't use some compassion?

Or from outrage to forgiveness. Who couldn't use some forgiveness?

Or from thanklessness to gratitude. Who couldn't use feeling some gratitude?

Perhaps even from discontentment to contentment. Who couldn't use feeling contentment where having all that we need to be happy is right here and right now?

You will be transformed!

22

The Pareto Principle

⊱⊰

Perhaps you've heard of the 80/20 rule: the principle used in business, industry, and many other disciplines. It is named after Vilfredo Pareto, a multi-talented Italian engineer. It is hard to believe the principle was derived partially from a garden. Yet we all know that good things come from gardens.

Not only do I believe this same rule applies to my backyard garden, but also to my closet. There is hardly room in there for more clothes, yet I seem to only wear about twenty percent of them.

Taking this principle into this century, what can be observed is that superficiality is rampant in our lives. Global information is persistently and repetitively thrust upon us, and we are on overload. We have generously taken this new, superior transmission of information in stride, for we love our smartphones, the marvelous World Wide Web, and social media, not to mention other instantaneous information sources allowing us to share way too much information twenty-four hours per day.

Can information come too quickly? Conflicting headlines just keep coming, and we find ourselves forced into making major decisions about what is happening in a world based solely on those headlines, often without knowing any of the story behind them.

We cannot stand in a line waiting for a coffee that we have already ordered online for more than ten seconds without bowing our heads towards our phone for the latest tidbit on someone's vacation or bad day. Perhaps we are posting because we have been forced to wait for coffee standing in a line?

Technology has delivered instant gratification to us, and we now crave it. We just cannot get enough. It is like a drug. The new alibi for real life. Instant on/off. We make sure to friend enough people to create our own personal instant audience. Someone is always online after all.

Traditional voice communications now take too long, so short texts suffice. Video clips advise of daily activities, and a tender thought produces a sweet quote someone else once said, coming to us with the directive to type Amen and share.

Though the argument can be made that we are staying in touch with folks for whom other means of communication are impossible, the concept here is about the time commodity and its implications on the whole of our lives. These media connections are inherently frivolous, and we know this to be true. We live them each and every day and wonder where the time went. We are easily bamboozled into letting go of precious time. Odds are we spend about eighty percent of our waking hours in this false environment.

This phenomenon screams that we are desperate and have an obsessive need to connect with each other in a real and human way. Remember Maslow and his hierarchy of needs? Belonging comes right after physiological needs and safety. We want to belong because we are human, and it is a basic need of our existence. Belonging means having deep connection, and since deep connections are not fleeting in nature, they do not come in one hundred forty characters.

Deep bonds take time. The time that is left over, that twenty percent, cannot possibly support or develop the rapport and relationships that are necessary for healthy human survival.

And in that twenty percent, is that where we live our spiritual lives? Is that leftover interval where we put our relationship with God? Only you can answer that question. Only you, on your singular journey can decide what is worth spending time on. On who is worth spending time with.

It is only time. But it is as precious as life itself. For life to be lived to its fullest, we need to make and keep those deeper connections to that which is most important to us.

So, what is the 80/20 of your life?

Henry David Thoreau once wrote, "It's not enough to be busy. So are the ants. The question is: What are you busy about?"

23

A Thousand Forks

༄༅

Life is filled with choices. To do right, to do wrong. To follow God in some way, or to choose not to and make your way in the world without Him. Did you choose the college path or go right into business? Perhaps you went a different way altogether at that time in your life. After college, yep, more choices. Life is filled with roads; some less traveled, and many very well-traveled.

Consider both fate and destiny. Do you, like the Greeks, believe that fate is something you just cannot escape? Fate for them was like an ethereal power that predetermined events in one's life. It seems that fate is about the bad things that happen in life. The three fates from Greek mythology were depicted as three women who controlled men's lives. Destiny, though a synonym of fate, is generally used to depict good things that happen. It is thought that man can influence destiny.

Since we are considering options here, how about free will. As Christians we are taught that free will is a wonderful, God-given gift. Not all religions believe we humans enjoy free will for it implies we have the ability to choose for ourselves. Ultimately our decisions are up to us and are not a foregone conclusion. There is power in choice.

Relying on fate rather than free will is easier than having to deal with the responsibility that free will creates. We all know there are consequences to every choice. So, let us talk about those consequences. Parents raise their offspring with stark and opposite choices: right and wrong, black and white, good and bad, and so forth. It is easier to teach children this way. Just punish the wrong choice. The difficulties come in as we mature, learn to make the decisions on our own, and learn life is more a complex shade a gray, rather than distinct black and white.

We could consider the perspective that no choice is a bad one. Each choice just reveals a different consequence. We are however virtually hard wired with the idea of morality which leads us to right and wrong as the only possible outcome of choices. Most of us, therefore, reject that viewpoint. Again, with maturity our decisions become based not only on the people we are striving to become, but also the people we expect others to be. Of course, this also plays into the kind of communities and nation we want to live in.

There are certain big choices in life. Where we choose to live. When and if to buy a house. What type of vehicle to purchase? What kind of job will fulfill and support us? Should we have children.

Let us consider the everyday choices we all make. For example, our thoughts and actions such as food, drink, what we read, who we befriend, our intentions for ourselves, our family, our behavior, and reactions to the world around us. What if these were more than just simple everyday decisions? What if these choices/decisions were actually the bigger, more important decisions of our lives?

What if our choices prevented us from moving forward toward enlightenment? What if our simplest daily choices kept us from being kind? What if our generally lousy attitude kept us from a compassionate response to someone who just lost a loved one? What if our daily choices prevented us from a closer relationship with God because we chose to ignore Him today?

What if we chose the left fork in the road tomorrow instead of the right for a change? Where might that take us? We do get to choose our thoughts as well as our every action and reaction.

Do we make the choices every day that leave us with a good feeling about ourselves? Let us be brave and find out. Let us confront ourselves, and our desire for integrity. Let us take back our power and choose to be who we have always wanted to become. Let us get a grip on our own senses of fairness, of honesty, and yes, kindness and compassion too. Those small, everyday choices are our true selves in action. Each of us anxious to see where the road leads and which fork we will take today.

24

Come Home

※

A few years ago, there was a conference I really wanted to attend but could not afford the tickets. The organization offered two free tickets for winning a writing contest that was held and judged weekly for a month leading up to the event. I was determined to win and had already told a friend of my intentions. Each week the theme was the same, to write about personal struggles one had overcome.

Giving it my all, week after week, and I did enter every week, I was disappointed that the tickets always went to someone else. When I read the winning essays however, I knew exactly why I had not won the prize. The narratives were all so much more dramatic and powerful than mine could ever be.

There were chronicles of daring escapes from dictatorial governments, long treks across scorching deserts dodging tyranny, and families traversing tempestuous oceans on makeshift rafts in search of new lives. Gut wrenching tales of life and death; of bravery and courage; of charity and openheartedness so grand they brought tears to the eye. Stories so incredibly remarkable that my little life paled in comparison. Even a prize-winning author would find it difficult to compete with the truths that were spoken in these persuasive experiential voices.

Yes indeed, I would have to buy those conference tickets as I was never going to win them. And so it is with life....

Someone else's experiences will always be bigger, more wonderful, or more harrowing. Their writing will be more eloquent, their faith seemingly stronger. It is true that we often see others as so much more than we see ourselves in this life. We have so much stuff around us and in our heads that instead of accepting what we have, we compare everything and are always striving to have more and better.

As children all we really needed was to feel safe, loved and protected. So how did we get here?

Sadly, we have forgotten the value of having those three things. We try. We know we should be grateful, so we make gratitude lists. Good start. But how about we start to live the gratitude? How about we come home to ourselves?

Only when we come home to our true selves, can we experience our fullest potential as human beings. This allows us to understand, and more importantly to feel and to know that who we are is enough.

We can come home to knowing that by being safe, being loved, yes, being loved by ourselves, and by being loved by God is enough. We do not have to deceive ourselves into believing there is more we need to do, need to have, or need to be.

Enough. What a beautiful word. Enough means more than sufficient, it also means plenty, abundant, plentiful, and ample. When we are enough for ourselves, we can start to see all the blessings God has laid out for us in our lives. And there are so many blessings!

I could never have won those tickets; neither based on talent nor horrendous experiences. Yet what I gained in hearing those stories helped me to feel blessed, despite what I had considered to be struggles in my life. I am learning to accept every day that I am enough.

I thank my Creator daily for keeping me safe, for protecting me, and for loving me always.

25

Your Garden Wall

⚘

Garden walls come in all types and sizes. Some are boundaries of rivers, fences, or trees, both natural and man-made. Beautiful and effective. Some inviting a closer look, while other walls are very foreboding. Much depends on what is going on inside that wall.

In a Soul Garden, the wall is the boundary of our soul's experiences and where we are willing and not willing to go. Soul Garden walls are similar to the ones we see marking property lines. Some are extremely tall and thick and offer extreme protection…the sole purpose of which is to keep people and experiences out. Some boundaries are simple picket fences. Friendly, and you can see through to the inside. Occasionally we will find Soul Gardeners with no boundaries at all.

Someday I hope to have a no boundary Soul Garden, but I still show intensely human qualities that cause me fear and doubt. And since I have not quite mastered living in the moment, which is the requirement of a 'no boundary' soul garden, I admit being pretty happy with what I believe to be my short picket fence.

Soul Garden boundaries serve as the filters through which we live and allow life. The mesh through which we see the world, as well as our fears, and our willingness to participate in the world. They represent the way we see ourselves. What we show as our soul garden wall is our sense of who we are and who we are not.

Should we, individually, be brave enough to question these boundaries, we will have the opportunity to change not only our core beliefs, but also the way we portray ourselves to the world. That actually will be a natural progression, for the wall, or lack thereof, represents how vehemently we protect our core beliefs.

Are we secure enough in our faith to be open to someone else's faith? Do we have friends of other faiths? Because another chooses God differently, does that change who we are? Will someone else's choices interfere with our values? Will another's perspective of the Lord somehow prevent us from having our own vision of Heaven?

This may come as a surprise, but every single member of our own churches has a different vision of God. Their life experiences, family life, joys and sorrows are not like ours, and they experience the Almighty with different perspectives. Some may see God as an old man with a beard, others as the energy that permeates the universe. Still others as may see Him their closest friend.

Let us not limit what and who God is to anyone. Instead, let us rejoice that He has been found...no matter the path.

26

Heart of Hearts

☙❧

To know something in your heart of hearts means that you truly feel or believe in it. So, when did you know that you were a believer? Whack! Right out of nowhere I ask one of the deepest, most personal questions. Yet I wonder if you remember when that was? Where that was? Was it a private decision or public?

Did you find Him on your own? Do you recall what made you curious enough to go and seek Him? How did you first bring God into your life? Have you ever thought of that experience again?

Perhaps you grew up in a faithful family of regular worshipers? Should that be the case, as in my family, the child just follows along and merely participates with the family traditions. It is simply understood what is expected of the children. There must be a time though, a moment, when you take the Lord into your own heart because you want Him to be there. You want the grace and the forgiveness to be a part of your soul.

Standard ceremonies become a part of our lives as we celebrate with friends and family. The festivities start taking place shortly after birth, then symbolic baptisms, ritual confirmations, the Lord's Supper, Holy

Communion, Passover, worship services, prayer meetings, other Sacraments, even marriage and death are filled with religious ritual.

Have you considered the true meaning of these events as you participate now as an adult? Perhaps you celebrate the holidays of a particular faith? Do you try to follow the commandments or the Mitzvoth? Do you follow the teachings of the Buddha, and want to revisit the five Precepts or the Noble Eightfold Path?

Oh yes, there are lots of questions to be found here today, and you are the only person who can answer them. At the heart of all these questions is for you to come to a personal understanding of where you are with your faith, and with your God.

The answers are simply opportunities to renew your faith with a new commitment to it and to God. Think about it. Sacraments and practices are thrust upon infants and very young people. We are born into those rites that happen very early in life, most to guarantee acceptance into the family of God, or in an attempt to provide entry into Heaven. Consider Catholic Holy Communion at seven, and Protestant confirmation or Jewish Mitzvahs at about twelve years of age. Young. And yes, tradition. We do teach the youngsters about this thing called faith, and we then consider them part of the faction. But then we let them go. Pushing them out of the nest and hoping to have made a lifelong impression. Can a commitment we made as a child really hold up through a lifetime?

Participating in religious ceremonies offers us many gifts. Beautiful ways to remember the lives of people we love; celebrations of life and love; joy; and, to remind us to practice our faith. Considering how our lives change in the many years we are blessed with this life; wouldn't you think that a reconfirmation of that childhood commitment to God would be particularly special?

After all, some couples get remarried after many years to recommit to each other and renew their vows. Why not a rebaptism of one's faith? A reconfirmation? You do not have to have a party, but you could. Just imagine the invitation. "Hey there, want to come over to my house for a party? I'm reaffirming my commitment to God and His commandments. It'll be fun!"

Ask yourself, "What do I really believe about God, religion, the Torah, the Bible, the Commandments, all the miracles? What are my true feelings and beliefs about this in my heart of hearts?"

Spend some time enlightening yourself. And when your heart of hearts is ready, recommit, and do it any way you would like. It is something you will never forget!

27

Golden Calf

෨ CB

A year or so ago I saw a bumper sticker that was a quote from the Dalai Lama. It said, "Kindness is my religion." Made me wonder what I would answer if asked what my religion is now. What I learned by asking others, is there are a few pat answers, including, 'I'm spiritual, not religious,' or 'I'm a recovering (fill in the blank)' or 'I used to be a (fill in the blank).'

This does not mean a person has no religion, because the definition is more than the belief and worship of an omnipotent power. Religion, you see, also defines the pursuit of that which is of supreme importance to the individual. In that case, we each do have an answer. It just might not have anything to do with God.

What do you pursue with all your heart and soul? Money? Love? Happiness? In this century, the answer could well be instant gratification or perhaps simply a strong Internet connection?

Could these be representative of a Golden Calf for our civilization? Are we consciously choosing to put our faith in external sources of pleasure and happiness?

It is easy to put our foundation in God aside. Many of us were taught that an hour once a week in nice clothes was all that was required. Others had confession and a list much longer than just Ten Commandments that had to be followed. Parents have used religion more as a threat and punishment rather than as a source of the peace and joy it could bring.

Makes sense that many leave that kind of religion behind, and in its place we gladly create a golden calf for ourselves. We tell ourselves that this is more satisfying, not realizing that the external sources of joy and happiness are short lived and hardly deeply fulfilling.

Our original foundation lies in wait for us to rediscover. This is the internal, personal joy that is found from bringing God into your heart and into your life. This is the love, the nurturing compassion, the forgiveness, and the grace that no golden calf can offer.

Consider what is of upmost importance to you. What do you truly live for?

Put God where He belongs in your life. Let Him speak to you and guide your comings and goings. He will speak to you in surprising and unexpected ways and fill you with a peace that truly passes all understanding.

28

The Foolish Gardener

❧☙

This gardener pretends that the introduction to religion in his childhood, the one perceived as too strict, a requirement of his parents, and not something he ever personally experienced, is all he needs to get through this life…and the next. He sees life as a competition because that's what society taught him. Consumerism is his social conscience, and God is a forgotten part of his past. He now lives and dies by social media; the latest in false prophets. Yet his life is empty of depth; void of true wisdom, and he doesn't even know it. Why? There is no self-insight. No depth of understanding. No discernment. No perception or awareness of what lies at his core, his foundation. The complexity of who he is and what his life is about is lost in the external spectacle of it all.

This hopeful but foolish horticulturist plants his seeds of desire only to be disappointed in how long it takes for them to sprout leaves for the gardener to relish and enjoy. Otherwise, what is there to show off? Here, tending to the garden is a chore to be endured. It is about showing off faith as confidence and conviction, but not quite every day, and not quite about God. These gardeners are proud of their accomplishments, their children, and their stuff. They may not show off materially, but one can tell that they delight in the jealousy and envy from others.

The foolish gardener believes his relationship with God need only be visited on big holidays, weddings, and funerals. He shows up because it is what is expected: a display for others. Like a bouquet of purchased flowers where no effort was put forth but to phone in an order, the showy flowers have no way to survive.

Compare the Soul Gardener delighting in even the idea of having a relationship with God. With this bond in mind, this gardener looks for kernels of relationship to gently place and tenderly nurture. Her self-insight means she has learned the seeds thrive first by driving their strong roots into the welcoming environment. The gardener knows these beginnings will create a foundation that will not only form the basis for her relationship with God as life grows and thrives, but also a foundation one can return to again and again if needed for support. The Soul Gardener is always building on a firm foundation.

This compassionate groundwork is laid by determining what her goals are for her Soul Garden. She wants a personal relationship with God and will nurture it so that it flourishes. A Soul Gardener has learned that a successful relationship requires transparency, communication, sacred space, and respect, so she plants those in her garden. Her insight focuses on what she can continually do to improve her relationship, and she knows herself very well...the good and the bad.

For transparency, she offers herself to God exactly as she is, sins and all. The gardener communicates with her Lord daily, often moment to moment. Her life becomes a prayer. She creates sacred space for her relationship. Private time to reflect on the grace she is given. Her respect and love for her God is unending and joyous.

Her seeds blossom into love. They express themselves as compassion. Daily, her gratitude is articulated, and peace is a cherished by-product. The Soul Gardener's harvest is unending as is His love.

May your garden be blessed.

29

Ignite a Fire in Your Soul

☙☜

Ever have a fire in your belly? You know, have a deep passion for something that you just cannot get out of your mind and heart until you do something about it. Of course, you have, we all get that at some point. It is an exciting, driving force that will take us down a road we just have to take, for as long as we 'feel' it. It is a sensation I want you to have again. I want you to ignite a fire in your soul for everything your life holds. The spark that will move you forward and propel you toward the best parts of being alive.

What if you had a fire in your soul for the Lord? Would that make you a zealot? Or would that make you look foolish? What does someone with a fire in their soul look like anyway? You might just want to check the mirror. It could be the person in that reflection. It may be a close friend. Is it?

You are not alone with these pent-up feelings. We are all over, even if not everyone knows it. Why? Because not everyone's personality is designed for standing on street corners, waiving Bibles, and preaching. Many of us just love loving God right here at home.

Besides, it is obvious that not all our friends and family are receptive to talking about spirituality, or miracles, or heaven, let alone God's whispers! We have such deep-seated fears of segregating ourselves from those we care about or love. We do not want to be apart from them...isolated or mocked. It is a giant step forward to our own growth in faith to try to talk to folks about this burning fire for Him.

Sometimes tragedy brings it out in us. We jump to pray with the nation for a shocking event. We long to send God's love to those affected, but then all too soon the world moves on forgetting the God part. And we move on as well, back into our protective shells where we feel loved and blessed by God but keep it all to ourselves.

I believe that our hearts and souls are looking for less drama, less time on smartphones, and more time enjoying the love of family and friends. I believe there is peace in love and compassion and that when we find it, we long for more and more of the same kind of happiness. Now that is something that can ignite one's soul!

This kind of joy can build a real fire inside a person to actively seek Him out more often. We may start to burn with compassion for the world. Put a match to forgiveness in our own life, and the lives of others while fanning the flames of desire for a place in heaven.

'I met someone once who inspired me.' 'I am reading a book about something worth mentioning to you.' 'I read a blog the other day that made me think.' All great opening lines to start a conversation with someone about a God who loves without end. The One who represents all that is wonderful in this life and the next.

So, while we are chatting here about this, have you thought about eternity lately? Bet the news has made you think a bit about life and death. The natural and unnatural disasters are bringing eternity to those who woke up that very morning without a clue that it would be their last day of life on earth.

Eternity is right here...perhaps a breath away. Let us not let our minds panic because they are afraid to look at the future we all hold.

As humans we know we won't get out of this life alive. But eternity? So how are we supposed to grasp eternity? Time unending? Everlasting? How are we supposed to prepare for something like that?

Wouldn't we rather have a little slice of heaven right here on earth than worry that there just might be a hell? It is easier to push God down a little further into ourselves because the thought of eternity is just too much to handle. It is not always easy to wrap our heads around these mysteries.

As God loving people, we are promised eternal life. Yet there are requirements for that everlasting heavenly life, and if preparations are still needed, do it now. Get right with God. In the future, may heaven be your home.

30

The Importance of Roots

ಬ ೧೩

The roots anchor the plants into the ground. They drop out of the seed or bulb first, to provide nourishment and stability prior to the sprouts that will head upwards toward the sun. Roots give plants a foundation upon which to grow and blossom. They draw up water and life sustaining nutrients so the plant may flourish against all odds. Little hairs grow off the larger root structures to take in even more nutrients and minerals from the earth so the roots can store energy.

Our human roots suggest where our ancestors began their journeys. Knowing that helps us to understand a bit more about ourselves and our families. These roots can help us to understand past generations by learning about the time periods and what was going on in the world at that time. Any such details will add color to the simple human struggles we all face and try to survive.

But we have Soul Garden roots as well that guide and protect. These are our deep and thoughtful beliefs. They are the values in which we find stability, even as we sometimes meander and push our way through our life.

Many of us have forgotten to take care of these Soul Garden roots. It is easy to lose our way at times. We often find ourselves surrounded by bad behavior, and can get pulled in. The deeper and stronger our roots grow, the deeper and stronger our foundation becomes, helping us to feel secure and safe.

These moral and incorruptible roots are the bedrock of our principles that we use to interpret and influence this world around us. We must feed the roots so that they will support growth and provide strength in the face of hard and tempting times. In life that could mean feeding the roots with faith, kindness, compassion, and forgiveness. The hardships of life, disease, job loss, depression, all need a strong basis for survival. We will look toward our foundation for strength, for self-compassion, for kindness.

Time to check the root system of our lives, my gardening friends. How is it doing? Roots healthy? Keep up the good work. Life not flourishing? Look deeper. Is your foundation supportive of your current condition? Should improvement be necessary, start with the roots. To combat despair, try cultivating hope and joy. To fight off anger, try humor. Unkindness: kindness. Lack of compassion: compassion.

These wonderful, loving qualities are what most of us admire and strive for. Let us make the better choices as we rebuild our root system. Roots need water or need nutrients? Add some love and share the joy.

A rich life flourishes with a healthy root system and strong values.

31

The Cleansing

෨ଓ

A nice hot shower, clean hair that smells oh so good... a warm, soft towel to gently collect the excess. Yes, that is what a gentle cleansing sounds like to most of us. We may think of Jesus cleansing us from our sins. We never think of that as a painful process for us: but more of a purification, something we long for...are promised as Christians...and that which will move us into the Heavenly realm.

Look up cleansing nowadays, and one learns about cleaning the human body from the inside out. Juice cleanses, liver cleanses, colon cleanses...Get rid of those toxins!

Do you think it is possible to have a culture cleanse? Could that be something we signed up for without even knowing it? When the number of events seems out of proportion, I tend to think there is something greater going on.

Taking a hint from the body cleanses, we would need to look at our culture's inner workings. Like the sexual harassment scandals? The persecution we impose on others who are not the same as we are? The mass shootings? The bullying? So many dirty little secrets are being exposed.

And yet there is even more going on. Hurricanes, flooding, fires, evacuations. Surely, we mere humans do not have power over Mother Nature. Yet while that is true, we do have the power to decide where homes and communities can and should be built.

The innocents are always sacrificed. When did we decide not to have compassion? Or is the better question, when did greed become our first choice? When a whole society gets a cleansing, there is not much comfort going around.

Perhaps it is finally time to address some obvious problems we have? Here's hoping we have had enough of the persecution and maltreatment we take out on each other.

Mother Nature can be wild in her outrage, and it feels we have mistreated the planet enough to enlist her rage. Could there be a Higher Power at work? No one knows for sure, but I would speculate as much.

Many turn to God in disaster, often by asking "Why me, Lord?" And just as often, true goodness and mercy comes plentifully from complete strangers. And after the panic? Where do we turn after?

People get religious during and for a short time after disasters...they go to church, they pray to God for deliverance from their trials, and their pain. But devotion goes missing within a few days or weeks. People move back into their busy lives, though often on a different tack. See ya later, Lord, I am back on my feet again!

Isn't it time to bring God into our lives before the storm? Could we use these opportunities to discover true spiritual comfort? Can we finally realize that a gentler, happier way to live does exist? Can being clean and fresh mean being able to take a deep breath and relax in the knowing that there is more that unites us than divides us?

Let us share how to have compassion. What respect for all life means. May we reach out to all without judgment. May the Lord bless and keep those suffering from our mistakes in judgment, and may He also be welcomed into our everyday lives once again.

32

Thanksgiving

⊰⊱

A recurrent theme – Thankfulness – and this time of year, practically a requirement since we hold a dinner called Thanksgiving! Just yesterday I read a quote from Paramahansa Yogananda that said, "You should be thankful for everything at all times." Where that may sound like a lot of work, it does not have to be.

It is easy to say 'thanks' for someone holding a door open, even when getting change from a purchase, but it doesn't seem to happen all that often anymore. We are all too rushed…too annoyed…too preoccupied to bother with hurried kindness. Adding some simple 'Thank You's' to our lives might be a nice way to end the year.

Think from the perspective that we are, who we are, always. If there is something we want to incorporate into our lives, we will find a way to do it. We generally add new habits gradually…as we may have to remind ourselves to think about it in the beginning, but it will soon become routine.

There are tangible benefits from genuine thankfulness. A heartfelt 'Thank You' elevates us and places us in a blissful state. Wholehearted thanks allows us to not only experience joy and appreciation emotionally, but also to feel contentment physically. Think about it. When were you last truly thankful? Did you notice the emotion? The feeling in your body? It is a shame that we have forgotten, for the most part, to even notice the most gentle and sweet feelings we can have from simple gestures.

Genuine thankfulness is fulfilling to our souls. Our bodies melt into thankfulness with a big sigh, creating a release from the tensions of life. It completes the cycle of want, of need, allowing our bodies to release stress — purging it from our muscles and cells.

We are talking about a precious moment of gratitude that is as physical as it is mental and emotional. It represents having enough – satisfaction — contentment. What a blessing to be able to experience all this and get a meal too!

No matter how you spend Thanksgiving Day...Here's wishing your gracious thankfulness brings your recipients and you, blessings you each can feel and enjoy! Happy Thanksgiving!

33

Why I Lied to My Minister

※

Going through confirmation in the Presbyterian Church required that all the twelve-year olds take several classes under the tutelage of our minister. Kilburn Memorial Presbyterian Church was the locale of the moderately interesting classes, that by the way, included homework! We were to learn about the beginnings of Presbyterianism and garner a healthy foundation in the faith. I am sure this included stories about the sixteenth century Protestant Reformation, and how the church was influenced by French theologian John Calvin, and a Roman Catholic Scotsman named John Knox.

However, there is one memory I have that is crystal clear. It is the day I lied to my minister. Why? Well, one of the homework assignments was to write a prayer: just like one I might say before going to bed at night. Simple, right? "Now I lay me down to sleep..."

In my childhood I learned to hold religion close to the vest because that is what I saw daily. People practicing their faith without obligation or fanfare. They simply loved and enjoyed their faith. My maternal grandparents were the driving force in a 'lead by example' sort of way. Church every Sunday morning, and prayer meetings some evenings. Faith demonstrated but neither forced nor extolled, save grace before every meal. The same one I use to this day. "Come dear Jesus, be our guest, and bless our daily food. Amen."

There were far lengthier versions of grace on major holidays when our home became the gathering place for all aunts, uncles, and cousins within a few hours' drive. I had all the experience I needed to do this assignment. I had listened to great prayers at home and at church.

And here I was, required to write out a prayer to the one and only God. The God I thought of as a personal friend... "What a friend we have in Jesus!"...and my personal Savior. That is the way I understood it anyway.

How could this man, a minister after all, ask me... require me, to put something so very personal on paper so he could read it. Nope, it was not going to happen! So, I lied. When called on it, I lied. I told him I had turned it in already. He knew it wasn't true, but for some reason let me slide. I was confirmed with full membership in the church. My coming of age church experience had a lie in it...

I was twelve. I could not possibly fess up to the truth. I could not tell that man that my faith was already very, very strong. I had lost a lot of family in those twelve years, and watched and learned that no matter what, through sickness and tragedy that the Lord was always with me.

My family talked to the Lord like a revered family member. They spoke with love and admiration. With compassion. With trust. Faith in my family, and in my world, is very, very personal.

I am not the one to call on to say a prayer out loud, even to this day. My prayers are typically pretty short, sweet, and to the point. They are filled with thanks and gratitude. And they are mine. Oh, occasionally I find myself filled with so much love that I can go on and on with Him. Sometimes I find myself so grateful I weep. But you know what? That's between me and Him.

However, you choose to pray, and I hope you do...early and often, as they say. Do it your own way. Do it based on the relationship you have with Him. As that changes, so will your prayers.

It's all good. It's all special. It's all love.

34

Merry Christmas

෩൫

Here we are, the week before Christmas: Many of us are on the last days of Hanukkah, some are ignoring the meaning of Christmas, and are instead aiding in the celebration of winter consumerism. Christians are celebrating the birth of the Messiah.

Unfortunately, many of us are suffering this year from having lost something or someone we miss dearly. And now with Christmas and Hanukkah already here it is particularly difficult for us to face all the joy that seems to surround us. We are feeling especially off kilter this year, and not sure what to do about it.

If not affected yourself, perhaps you know someone who lost a friend or relative recently; the grief for them feeling unbearable. Horrible hurricanes in the Southeast United States were tragic enough yet are a vague memory for those only hearing about it on the news. Those who suffered through them are still fighting daily to get their lives back in order; their homes into livable condition; and their families able to sleep through the night.

The northern California fires were terrifying. Whole neighborhoods exploding in the firestorm. Families lived there. Loved ones. Beloved pets. Industries were destroyed.

And at the same time wildfires blew through Montana, devastating hundreds of thousands of acres.

And now, the southern California fires continue to burn, with thousands evacuating. The Santa Ana winds just refusing to die. More families, homes, pets, livelihoods. How many facing Christmas now homeless and traumatized?

If you have been affected by any tragedy this year, God Bless You in your recovery. No matter what you have suffered, talking about it is probably the last thing on your mind. But you need to heal from the loss, and that means you need to talk about it. Let people minister to you with kindness, offerings of food, money, or a listening ear.

Those not affected need a way to help. One way is to offer to be with those affected, providing a comforting presence. A kind word or two would be appreciated.

The Blessings of Christmas are these personal offerings – the kindnesses – the generous emotions shared – the displays of love. At the least, offer your prayers for their healing. Asking God to bless them is no small contribution. What a blessing to be prayed for after all...

And while we are at it, let us not forget the forty odd million people in the United States who are living beneath the poverty level. Somewhere along the way we screwed up, and we need to make it better somehow. Healing the homeless and poverty stricken will take time. Let us give these folks a God Bless too!

Think of Jesus on His birthday. How would He ask that you help the hungry, the sick, and the lonely? It is Christmas.

However, you choose to share your Blessings this beautiful season – May you also be mightily Blessed.

35

Christmas Eve

✺☙

As I consider Christmas's past, I remember the old-time songs. The hymns that we played and sang around the house all December long. Unlike the rest of the year, Christmas brought an abundance of music into our home.... into the car...outside...just everywhere! It was the time of 33 RPM LPs, and I was elected as the one to move the needle onto just the right place to start off the album, and to pull it off at the end of the stack of records, as the automatic feature didn't always work perfectly. More than likely it didn't work because we stacked too may Christmas albums on the spindle.

There was always a fresh Christmas tree in our home. One purchased as soon as the lots opened but put up on Christmas Eve. It seems that every year we suffered from the same memory problems, probably because we were all so excited. When we shopped for the Christmas tree in the cold outdoors, we could never really remember that our ceilings at home were only eight feet high. This was not always revealed immediately upon returning home, as we would put the tree in a bucket of water in the garage. There is where the second annual lapse of memory came into play. We would somehow forget that the water froze in that bucket each year... with the tree and the bucket firmly or frozenly, attached, of course.

Eventually, we would somehow get the bucket off, and the ice removed from the tree's stump as well. Warm water and a small hatchet were often employed. And chances were that someone would grab a hand saw and decide to not only freshen the cut on the bottom of the tree, but also make the tree shorter to fit in our home.

Long story short, it rarely ended up as a straight cut. So, the challenge then became to stand the tree in its stand, so that it was as close as possible to perpendicular to the floor. There were years we had to wire the tree to the wall to make that happen...

Then came the lights! Strung out across the living room floor to make sure they worked, replacing bulbs that hadn't made it, and hunting down the extension cord that would surely be needed. The tree was then lovingly decorated with as many lights as it could hold. Big bulbs, the kind that got hot!

And then, my grandparents' ornaments from the early nineteen hundreds were gently hung on the boughs, as well as more modern ornaments; and always the glass ones. The final touches were the garlands of 1" glass ornaments that swirled around the tree in graceful loops.

Don't you know, we would then remember we hadn't put the top on the Christmas tree!

Oh yes, the memories are more than grand, and I have pretty much remembered all the fails, and try not to repeat them. But I love the memories. The Christmas tree faux pas. The family gatherings. Midnight services on Christmas Eve; singing Silent Night in a darkened church with only the Christmas tree lights on. And of course, the dearly departed family and friends who had brought life and love to our past holidays. The feeling of joy and celebration, for our King was born this night, in the city of David, called Bethlehem.

May hope and love fill your homes, and the true joy of Christmas be in your hearts. And may this Christmas bring you many blessings.

36

It Is a New Year!

൝ CB

In this New Year, I am a new person. We all seem to want to start afresh and see the world with new eyes. We long to get started with the resolutions swirling in our heads for days.

What frightened me, I will conquer. What I avoided; I will tackle head on. I will be a better person this year because I will remember what is truly important, and I will live that truth every day. All so familiar. Such wonderful intentions. Blessings to you that you will succeed!

Where we welcome the celebrations and fresh start of any New Year, it feels like a good time to reflect also; not in sadness or regret, but in truth to what the past year has meant, personally, professionally, familywise, etc. And where necessary to let go of actions, disappointments, or sadnesses that have stayed with us longer than we truly needed them to hang on. For it is in the letting go, the releasing, and the forgiving that allows us to start the new season with promise, with joy, and with possibility.

No matter how we approach the New Year, whether looking forward, or taking a glimpse of the past, what we are all really looking for is happiness. At some point we determine that the joy we are pursuing is more internal in nature, and if we are willing to admit it, that kind of deep, rich, contentment is more spiritual than anything external. This evolution changes our actions, and the way we look at others.

This is how we grow, and isn't it the growing that changes everything? Let us grow with the hope that is born in the deepest, most vulnerable part of ourselves. Let us thrive with joy and love and abandonment. Let us prosper in the Light that grows stronger every day.

In this blessed New Year, may we let go of those things that hold us back from new experiences and joyfulness, and may we immerse ourselves in the wonder of all God's creations.

It is time again for me to handover my life to Him... to make my intentions for the New Year known. As in the prayer of Jabez who called upon the Lord asking to be blessed and have his territory increased, Jabez also asked that the Lord's hand might be with him always and keep him from all evil. God granted the requests.

So, with this blessed new beginning, let us make our intentions known to Him that He may bless our comings and our goings. And may the Lord bless you and keep you in this New Year!

37

Belief in God

❧❦

Religion and love are two of the greatest mysteries of this life. With each we must learn to trust and believe without any empirical evidence.

As humans we have a need to belong whether as a member of a family, a religion, or the fan base of a sports team. With belonging we are not only a part of something larger, but we also learn to feel safe and supported by others who have some of the same beliefs, values, or desires that we have.

There is also a downside to belonging. What the group does not believe in or does not understand, the group may criticize or even demonize, and fellow members will back up those opinions.

Our belief in God is one small step in the greater experience of faith. Having faith is a commitment of more than an hour a week hearing a sermon and singing a few songs. It is more than a television show hearing of someone else's devotion to Him.

Faith is giving up the idea that we must face all our problems alone. It is forever abandoning our fear of not being loved. Faith should be the tenet what we build our lives on.

What must we be telling ourselves if we do not have that conviction? That we are not good enough? That we are afraid? Or that our faith is just not that strong?

Habits and beliefs are hard to break. We are telling ourselves stories about how the world is filled with evil and greed, and then that is the way we see our lives. Should we tell ourselves that the world truly is filled with God loving, devoted people, our perception of the world changes.

That sounds simple, does it not? To simply put on a pair of rose-colored glasses and see the world as loving and kind. The concept is easy. The change is not.

As for soul gardening, we do grow what we plant. We may start with a belief that God exists, but there are many ways for that idea to blossom.

The belief in God can grow to where we believe He is everywhere and has created everything in this world. Our trust in Him can be cultivated to where we allow Him to guide and protect us. If we nurture our foundation of belief, we can develop our confidence in the Lord to a point where we trust completely in His loving care of our best interests. We can accept the Lord's promise to be with us always. Our devotion can enable us to feel peace, comfort and happiness from His love.

Belief in God can quickly change into loving God that will affect our lives greatly.

Now is the time to search and the time to challenge what you know about Him, and what you may still need to learn. Loving God says that not only do we believe in Him, we also trust in Him.

The Bible says to knock, and the door will be opened to you. The challenge to transform our belief into love is worth it. Life will still happen...the good and the bad. There are blessings and hardships along the way, but with the Lord at the center of our lives there can also be comfort. There can be joy, and there can be that inner peace that we all want to find.

We can begin by simply asking Him to guide our journey and open the doors to our understanding.

38

The Seeds of Desire

ॐ ও

Time to start seeds for the spring! How wonderfully easy would it be to just get a pound of magic seeds, and get each of them to blossom into whatever it is we want to grow? No special treatment, and no planting rules. These five will be tomatoes, these ten will be tulips, etc.

It would save the effort it takes to have to pick out individually what we want to see in the garden, and tenderly plant each at the right time, the correct depth, and with just the proper amount of sunlight and water. But then, something would be missing. The excitement to select just what we want to grow, and to nurture each exactly the way it should be cultivated.

What is at the heart of our desire is to follow God's path, making us a more giving and more loving person. This is often a very difficult path to follow. We have our minds and hearts set on this new, more spiritual way of being, and we cannot quite pull it off. It is as if our bodies are pre-programmed to do what we have always done rather than adapt to our new desires.

Why can't we just desire to change and have it be so? Why can't this change of heart make an immediate difference in our actions? Our subconscious beliefs and values are the reason we cannot just snap our fingers and change our behavior. Just like those seeds, we cannot wish them to be something they are not.

Our subconscious works like a navigational force that follows the direction given to it by our core principles. No judgment is offered by this internal system, our subconscious is just following orders given by our core. The subconscious says, 'you know what you want, and I'm just leading you down the path you said you desired.'

The seed destined to be a weed cannot have its path in life altered. A different seed is needed to become a rose. A core belief that one is unlovable, needs to be replaced with the core belief that one is lovable. That is how to open the door to healthy, loving relationships.

We have many seeds growing in our belief system, and sometimes they need to get changed out. We always need to plant the seeds we want growing and blossoming in our life. It may not seem fair, but those original seeds are created from early life experiences, relationships, upbringing, hopes, fears, God/no God instruction…you name it. It is our job as soul gardeners to figure this out and do something about it, especially if the seeds need replacing.

Planting healthy seeds of belief in children is so very important. Teaching them they are loved, capable, and able to overcome adversity is a blessing that will last a lifetime. Teaching them about God and His love is a beautiful gift to give them.

I had the blessing to have grandparents who loved the Lord, and demonstrated with every action, the love they felt for Him. That taught me early on to trust and believe in Him.

As adults we can now see how very difficult it is to change things in our lives, even when we want to react in a different way than we have in the past. Often it takes a good deal of introspection; figuring out just what those core beliefs are and perhaps where they came from.

The way we react every day to issues, people, or situations, is a perfect reflection of our personal, fundamental principles delivered right to our doorstep by our subconscious. All those principles, of course, our choosing.

Is it time to change out some of the seeds of belief in your life? What a perfect time to dig down and find the seed(s) that need replacing. Time to be open and positive and find a new seed to nurture. Do not forget to be patient and loving.

Try planting the seeds of desire to know and love the Lord. With seeds of trusting Him planted along side, both should flourish easily. It will be spring soon enough. Let us get a good root system started!

39

Everlasting Love

～☙☙～

Most people claim a belief in God. Yet we inherently disagree about what believing in God means. Our views are complex because we weave elaborate theories in our minds about life and how God fits into that. Our behavior is indicative of these theories. Some think God has little to do with how we behave.

Many of our conclusions are contradictory of each other. What is true for so many of us is that believing in God is not always easy. It does not help that the clergy as well as the liturgy can be confusing, and the Bible contains contradictions too. Are we at a place where two people believing in God do not have much in common?

We are afraid to delve too deeply into these principles because it frightens us to challenge what we believe. We allow each paradox to exist but are unsure what to do when we run into them head on. So, we slip and slide around them. It is just too intimidating, so we avoid talking about God.

Perhaps we should begin with our own perception of God. Is He the Creator of the heavens and the earth? Where is God now? Is God an old man with a white beard sitting on a throne somewhere in Heaven? Is God hard to find or easy? How do we know He really exists? Maybe there is no such thing as a Creator, let alone a loving source to all there is?

Finding a deeper love and understanding of God has more to do with our own truth than everyone else. So, what do your beliefs in God entail? No one will judge your perceptions, but this exercise may help you understand yourself in ways you cannot even imagine at this moment.

Go ahead and lay it on the line, list the fears and hopes you have accumulated about God. Search earnestly for the answers you need for your life, and for your love of the Lord.

You may write that He is loving, generous, and kind. But at times you see Him as vindictive because you lost someone you loved, and you blame the Lord for the loss?

Is God the fire and brimstone God of the Old Testament for you? Or maybe the loving character of Jesus in the New Testament?

If you have tried to get to know Him, perhaps your views are that He is all seeing and all knowing; that He is the creator of all and filled with grace and mercy. But even this definition is just words.

When any words become what you believe, they develop into self-fulfilling beliefs. They are the basis for how we perceive the world. The beliefs are the reason for behaviors, reactions, opinions...

Do you see the world as a frightening and scary place? Do you think people are out to get you? Or do you see the everlasting beauty in a world God created for you? Do you start with compassion or cynicism? Do you have forgiveness in you for others, and for yourself?

These questions are just the beginning, but they start with your perceptions, awareness and belief in your God. This is where your entire world can change.

P.S. Our understanding of God has everything to do with how we behave.

40

Beyond the Five Senses

☙❧

Time and space, as well as our five senses help us to perceive the world we live in. Humans, we are told, are unable to comprehend infinity. Both eternity and infinity are defined as something that goes on forever and ever. Endlessly. It is difficult enough to comprehend the size of our universe, so how do we understand what we cannot see or touch?

We can understand how far one mile is. It fits into our understanding. The moon is more than two hundred thousand miles away from Earth, and the sun is more than ninety million miles away. While we can see them, we have no real concept of their size. And the distance is nearly impossible to imagine. So how are we to fathom huge planets floating in space, or the Milky Way, or other galaxies, when astronomers can only relate to them in light years? What is a light year anyway? These are difficult concepts for the human mind. There is no reference point for infinity allowing us to grasp the idea.

The five senses we were taught about as children contribute greatly to our survival and perception of the world. Personal experience with them and the way our bodies work, provide us an awareness of our surroundings, and help us understand our physical restrictions. Sight and hearing have been studied in immense detail, as have taste, smell and touch. We have learned to enhance sight with microscopes and telescopes. And hearing can be improved and augmented in many ways. Get rid of smell, and taste becomes drastically inadequate. Touch is multifaceted, involving not only the perception of touching something, but the ability to feel texture, pressure, the awareness of itching, and the sensation of different temperatures.

Humans possess many more than five senses. We know when our bodies are moving, and where our arms and legs are at any given time. We can tell when the weather is going to change, and we can feel pain.

The sense that we all have, and sometimes like to pretend we don't, is intuition. It is that gut feeling that hits us from out of nowhere. That very personal and deeply instinctual feeling that tells us something is going to happen, or that another person has good or bad intentions.

My friends will tell you that their gut is never wrong... that they just know. And should one of them get a sense that a deal is bad, that a person is bad news, or something wonderful is going to happen, that gut feeling is what they will rely on every time.

When we need to make a decision, we may rationalize, or we may overthink. We may forget that we can trust our wise, true self. Of course, we may ask God for His assistance. Tell me, Lord, what should I do?

Just like the saying, trust your gut, there is something deep inside of us that is smarter and wiser than our conscious mind. Some say that intuition is a way that God speaks to us.

41

God is Limitless

☙❧

We set limits on our world for many reasons, but mainly to control our environment. Living in a finite world makes us feel more comfortable in it. Control, after all, means power, and power grants us influence and/or authority. And don't we all want some of that?

There are age limits, speed limits, size limits and more. There are upper limits, and cost limits as well. All ways to curb and restrict.

We limit ourselves for a million reasons. Many of them have to do with fear, like when we are afraid of punishment or of getting injured. Boundaries can be used to protect people or stop an action or behavior we are not willing to put up with.

We put a cap on our imagination for many reasons as well. Perhaps someone else shut down our ideas in the past, and we turned our creativeness off?

What we should never put limits on is our perception of God. Far too often we try to relate to God as a human person rather than as an omnipotent force. God is truly limitless. His love for each of us is immeasurable. His grace; His choosing to bless us despite our behavior, is genuinely benevolent. Yet how can we grasp such things when our human experience is so limited?

Faith. Complete trust in Him. Understanding that we may not have the ability to completely grasp all things God. We still have confidence in His promises, and therefore we trust. Our dedication and belief in the Word and the Power of the Lord can become the center of our existence. It is from that place of faith, we are able to face our human world with more love and, therefore, with more empathy.

Let us learn to pray in limitless fashion. Though we may still request money to fix the car, or for a miracle healing, or for someone to love. Let us not limit the amount of His blessing, nor tell Him how we want things to happen in our lives. Let us ask Him to continue to bless us in such a way that we are shown how to overcome all of our struggles. Let us ask Him to show us how to love, and how to better take care of ourselves and others?

Let us never limit the gifts that God is eager to bestow upon His children. May we be receptive to His love everlasting by opening our hearts to His love, His guidance, and His generosity. Just ask and allow His blessings to flow.

May you continue to be truly blessed.

42

Billy

~~~~

This past week we lost a Christian soldier, the Reverend Billy Graham. He was a shining star amongst evangelists and has often been called America's Pastor. He came into my life when I was a small child. My grandparents loved to watch his crusades on the one television we had in our home. Always with Bible in hand, Billy, as he loved people to call him, gave us the gospel with a heart filled with love for the Lord.

Billy asked us to surrender to Him from no particular church's dogma. He spoke from his heart in a warm and genuine manner. He asked that we take that moment to repent of our sins; to accept Jesus as our Savior and be born again. Billy told us that if we would just say yes to the Savior tonight, in a moment we would know comfort. He always asked the masses to come forward at the end of his sermon and commit their lives to Jesus. And then the choir would start singing, "Just as I Am." And the people came to the pulpit and met the Lord for the first time.

Oh, I can hear the singing now. I just love the old hymns best! Each night we watched I would accept Jesus all over again, knowing that those lyrics were meant for me. And I would repeat the prayer Billy told me to say out loud. And

I would do it again today if Billy Graham were preaching. He just had a way of letting you know that this would be the best decision of your life.

"Just as I Am" is a song that invites us to realize that God will accept us just as we are...sins and all. The humbling lyrics go like this:

> "Just as I am, without one plea,
> But that Thy blood was shed for me,
> And that Thou bid'st me come to Thee,
> O Lamb of God, I come! I come!"[3]

It is impossible for me to get through that one without welling up a bit...even today as I type. The memories are so great and so dear of my grandparents who taught me about my faith.

It was through those crusades that I was introduced to songs like "How Great Thou Art"[4] long before Carrie Underwood made it famous once again in 2008. My whole family loved it, and it was sung at my mother's funeral. Listen to it soon. If you know the Lord at all, it will fill your heart with love, and remind you of the abundance that the Lord has put here for you. The first verse goes like this...

> "O Lord my God! When I in awesome wonder
> Consider all the worlds Thy hands hath made.
> I see the stars, I hear the rolling thunder,
> Thy power throughout the universe displayed.
> Then sings my soul, my Savior God, to Thee:
> How great Thou art, how great Thou art!
> Then sings my soul, my Savior God, to Thee:
> How great Thou art, how great Thou art!"

This small tribute to the Reverend Billy Graham is a reminder to me of those early childhood days where I first learned about God and Jesus. A time when I could never have realized what an impact all of it would have on my life, and how much the Lord would be blessing me. As I share my life's experiences with you, I too would love nothing more than for you to receive the Lord's blessing.

"Softly and Tenderly"[5] is yet another invitation to come home to our Lord.

"Softly and tenderly Jesus is calling
Calling for you and for me
See on the portals He's waiting and watching
Watching for you and for me.
Come home, come home
Ye who are weary come home.
Earnestly, tenderly Jesus is calling
Calling, "O sinner come home."
O for the wonderful love He has promised
Promised for you and for me
Though we have sinned He has mercy and pardon
Pardon for you and for me.
Come home, come home
Ye who are weary come home
Earnestly, tenderly Jesus is calling
Calling, "O sinner come home"
Come home, come home (come home)
Ye who are weary come home
Earnestly, tenderly Jesus is calling
Calling, "O sinner come home"

43

Last Words

୧੦੦੪

We have all had times or moments when we were frightened for our very lives. Frightened out of our minds. The one event for me happened on a ski trip to Colorado. It was one of those perfect winter days. The Earth resting beneath the glistening snow. The bluest possible sky with a glorious sun beaming what little warmth we could feel on the mountain top. A fresh layer of powder on the slopes. It was a skier's delight.

It was a mid-February semester break, and a friend and I were in line again at the chair lift after a few outstanding runs already. Couple by couple, we worked our way to the double chairlift where each person lined up their skis in the tracks of those who came before. This was back in the day, prior to snowboarding! As the lift comes up from behind, each skier turns slightly to line up with the chair. The chairlift is attached to the cable that will pull us up the mountain, by a metal rod in the middle of the two seats.

This one time, my college buddy, did not get her skis into the far tracks where they belonged...she was in my tracks. And as the chair came around, she quickly scooted into the correct tracks and seat, leaving me a step behind. Fortunately, she made it into her chair, but I ended up with my bottom straddling the outside arm of the lift. So as the lift ascended and took its normal first bounce, I did not bounce into the chair, I bounced out.

There I dangled, clinging desperately to that center pole with both hands. My ski poles dropped from my hands, and my skis left their bindings dangling from my boots with their safety straps doing their job. My friend turned and yelled at the life operator, as did the people on the chair behind us, to no avail. Now, I have never been a person of great upper body strength, nor have I ever been a small person, so this was even worse than it first seemed.

I saw huge brown boulders sticking up out of the snow below me, and panic overtook me. We were probably twenty-five feet or so in the air by then. I gripped that bar as tightly as I could and prayed, "God, help me!"

If all went well, there was a small bar beneath the chairs that would allow us to comfortably rest our skis on the ride up the mountain. I did not have the strength to pull my body up into the chair but did manage to get a boot on that bar. By the very Grace of God, by the end of the ride, I used that little piece of metal to hoist most of my body up into the chair.

My boots remained unattached from my skis, and I was noticeably shaking as I rolled off the ski lift in a clumsy dismount from the chair lift on the mountain top. My life had been spared by Him. There is no other explanation for me not smashing into those rocks.

Retrospection is a wonderful thing. And in this case, I have my great joy to even have had a life after that ski trip. More than that I find myself grateful that what could well have been my last words were, "God, help me" and not some spectacular exhibition of expletives! My terror reached down into my heart and called to God for help. I feel privileged, to know that I have Him there.

He is first in my life, and exactly where I want Him to be, and I guess you can say this event helped me to prove it to myself. My question now is, where is God in your life? Do you desire to have Him in your heart and to put Him first? And, in the end, what would you want your last words to be?

44

Confirmation Bias

Everyone has an opinion. I do not think that has ever been clearer than now. It doesn't matter whether we are speaking of politics or religion or whether a dress on the Internet is white or blue. And it doesn't even matter if someone asks our opinion: We have one. We not only give it freely on social media, but we also long to argue about it. Let us just say we overshare just about everything.

I heard Dr. Phil ask a guest on his show, "Do you want to be right, or do you want to be happy?" Do not be fooled, it is a trick question. Being right has taken on a whole new place in our world, or does it just seem that way to me?

Perhaps there was just a lot of drama in my childhood, but I am not a fan. Nor am I a fan of arguing. I would be pretty happy in a Utopian world, I think. It is not that I don't have an opinion...I have many. Often too many. I like to state what I think, but having knockdown, drag out arguments about them is not my first choice. It is not like I always lived like this. I had to learn to live here, but I love it.

I can actually enjoy other people's perspectives and opinions and religions and politics. I want to learn what others have to teach me that I am unaware of...or that I have previously rejected for myself. I had to learn to fight confirmation bias.

Confirmation bias is a human evolutionary trait. We are motivated by a desire to maintain the beliefs we already have, so we interpret the world based on that motivation. We cannot help ourselves. We automatically pay more attention to that information that supports our currently held opinions and disregard the rest.

Now it is one thing to take suggestions about your garden. Say someone at your local nursery advises putting two tablespoons of Epsom Salts around your roses and watering them deeply for bigger blooms. You may never have heard of that but might not think it a big deal to give it a try.

What if a Buddhist suggested you give up God, and your belief in one life on Earth, and just admit that all of life is about suffering? And don't forget you must now believe that reincarnation is real, and in the end our ultimate goal is Nirvana? Would you be as quick to give that a try?

Okay, so perhaps that is a drastic example of confirmation bias...but it works. Try this: What if your doctor, again through years of experience, believes your diagnosis should be the flu, and saw all of your symptoms as pointing to that? Fine if she's right, but what about the strong tendency to disregard the symptoms that point in another direction? Can you see where we need to be aware of this trait?

It will be a fight; I can promise you that. Much of what we believe was created and nurtured during our childhood. Think about it. It is the way we were built. It is the way we learned to survive.

We are now grownups, and we believe we are objective and that we use our years of experience to discern new information. But we are not as open to new ideas, new theories, and new perspectives as we want to think! The good thing is we know about confirmation bias now. Awareness can help us to challenge the concept and understand what is happening.

Let us do some Soul Gardening. Consider an exploration of some of your deeper beliefs. Reflect on how you feel about the Lord. Contemplate what it would take to expand your faith. Study how to turn your belief in God into a relationship with Him. How could one build a connection there? How is your rapport with Him?

So much to think about. So many reasons to do it. It is sure good to know that door is always open...

45

A New Hope

○○○

It is the first Palm Sunday, and Jesus is triumphantly entering Jerusalem on the back of a borrowed donkey. He sits on the cloaks of His disciples who have thrown them over the back of a donkey for Jesus to sit on. Multitudes welcome Him, laying their own robes down as well as branches of palm trees on His path into the city. The populaces hail Jesus as their King, coming in the name of the Lord.

This entrance into Jerusalem was the public announcement and the fulfillment of the Old Testament prophecy. If only the people had seen Him as their spiritual Savior...if only. But that was not to be. Instead they saw Jesus as the one who would lead them against Rome. And when that did not happen, and happen immediately, those same jubilant people turned on Him.

Look at our own world now. We turn our opinions over on a dime. We love one minute and hate the next. Are we attached to anything for the long haul?

The citizens of Jerusalem needed and wanted hope, yet they wanted only one kind of deliverance. What kind of hope do you need? What kind of confidence? Optimism? Courage? Faith?

Jesus was a different kind of hope. One that would provide much more to them than their earthly needs, but they could not see that for their pain from the oppression of Rome.

It has been said that if one is in their pain, their misfortune, that it is hard to find God, even if He says He is with us always. We are instead buried in our physical world and have forgotten His promise to us – to be there for us at all times. He is waiting you know, for us to accept His grace and tender mercies.

We hope for an end to our physical and emotional pain just like the residents of Jerusalem. We want what we want and not necessarily what is being offered, even though the offering is so much better. This is our challenge in life. To accept the journey through our physical existence and into the spiritual. It is all part of the great mystery of life. What we need is a new hope.

A hope for more than the end of the hurt we feel. A new hope for us to find peace, unending grace, and mercy. A new hope for the love that can only come from our beloved Father.

With Easter fast approaching, let us find this new hope in the celebration of the resurrection of our Lord Jesus. May you be blessed this Easter and always with the promise of everlasting life with Him.

46

Springtime

☙☛

Whether you think of spring as following winter or preceding summer, springtime has definitely arrived. Rebirth and resurrection are as much a part of the Easter season as they are of spring, reminding us to begin again the growth and renewal of our gardens and our souls. The vernal equinox marks the start of the season, as the Earth begins to increase its tilt relative to the Sun. The trees start to look green again as the tiny leaves burst out of the limbs that were bare just moments ago. The flowers bud and bulbs take root. It won't be long before the Earth becomes a kaleidoscope of color.

Our bodies experience the changes happening all around as the Earth warms and daylight seems to last forever. Many of our senses feel amplified hinting to us to make changes of our own. Plant something, release lady bugs, have flowers in the house again, spend more time outdoors. Just do something because it is time for everything to come to life again.

Consider some spiritual growth by doing some meditation or prayer or even some gardening. Did you know that gardening releases tension and promotes a person's longevity? It does. Just imagine what soul gardening can accomplish.

Finding it difficult to meditate and quiet the mind? Try thinking about God. I find that soothing because the topic is so much bigger than anything else I know, and I find myself in awe. That kind of amazement obscures any other thoughts I might have, and I find myself at peace.

Is it difficult to find what to say when you pray? Start with everything you are grateful for. Or begin with appreciation for all that He created for us to enjoy.

This time, any time, spent making a stronger connection to our Source is valuable. It builds our personal bond, and therefore our relationship with God becomes more intimate. And who doesn't want a closer walk with Thee?

This practice of spending time connecting to Him, brings us into the now. The present moment. This is where we truly need to learn to live, in the here and now. Compare that to our tendency to carry old baggage with us. Whether it is emotional or physical, it hinders our Earthly life and our spiritual one as well.

We need to let go of the past and focus on the present. Forgiveness is one of the most powerful processes we humans have control over. It is intentional and voluntary, and it is as cleansing to our emotional well-being as a soothing spring rain is to our gardens. It is a gift we give ourselves.

Practice giving forgiveness with your meditations and prayers. And then practice it again and again until you succeed in eliminating old painful emotions. Forgiveness is not a one-shot deal. Instead it is something that takes time and work. It is as physical as it is emotional. So, give yourself time and patience.

Wish those you have forgiven well. Move on into the present, the now, with a new attitude that has said goodbye to resentment, anger, and hurt.

Congratulations. You did not change the past, but you did change your future.

47

Take My Hand

ଛଠ

There is a popular video on YouTube depicting a speech given by Denzel Washington about "Putting God First." It is profound and beautiful. One watches for a few minutes or so, and spends another two minutes thinking about the words, and then what? Life goes on to the next thing.

Maybe we then check social media, or the phone rings, or perhaps we text someone to watch that video because it did strike a chord with us. Maybe we think about it one more time, and then what?

Life again. That pervasive calling to do something else. Multitask if at all possible. Control someone or something. We have succeeded in getting on with life. This is our world…and we love it as much as we complain about it.

But something about that video sticks in our minds. Something we would like to do, to put God first in our lives. But we feel it would take too much time or perhaps too much effort. And that is true if only because we are not sure of the next steps, because, after all, we do not want to get it wrong.

We want God in our lives more. He is there a little, for the occasional weekend service, the grace prior to a holiday dinner, maybe a sporadic "Now I lay me down to sleep," but not present in our day to day hectic lives.

How do we take on something as big and as auspicious as God, and squeeze that into our day? There is work or the kids, or all our other commitments. And the family must eat. The chores have to get done. The "to do" and the "honey do" lists are endlessly time consuming, and utterly impossible already.

We want to figure out how to put God first, and we just cannot wrap our heads around it. And that is the problem. We are using the wrong means.

This is the 24/7 commitment we want to make, and one that we fear. The Lord tells us at least four times in the Bible to love the Lord with all that we are. These are the words from Deuteronomy 6:5, "And thou shalt love the Lord thy God with all thy heart, and with all thy soul, and with all thy might." The words tell us how to do it. Rather than figure it out with our minds, we need only to make room for Him in our hearts.

Is there room in our hearts for love? Of course, there is. Can we ever have enough love? No, we cannot have enough love. Can we accept the unending, unconditional love that God offers? Are we willing to choose to let that love into our hearts and our lives? Once we allow ourselves to feel it, we will never let it go. We will carry it and feel it every hour of our lives. The proviso? We have to be open to letting that love in.

Once we do this, we will have begun our personal relationship with Him. Of course, we will want to find new ways to communicate and think of Him, whether to express our gratitude, ask for guidance, or request forgiveness. The bond becomes stronger over time, and suddenly we will find that He is in our heads as well as in our hearts...that place that had no idea how to find room for Him previously.

We will find the unrestricted love that only our Lord can offer. We might even ask for Him to take our hand and guide us through this life, like the hymn, "Precious Lord, Take My Hand."[6]

48

Embracing God

~~~~

This is truly what Soul Gardening is all about: Embracing God. Yet does this seem too great a desire? In the last chapter, we ended by asking God to take our hand, and guide us. For many of us, that may have begun a personal relationship with Him. And even if we have already had that belief and trust, we still long to find something that will bring us closer: something that truly embraces God.

I grew up in a Christian family. I saw pictures of Jesus often, and everyone in my family had a Bible, and a cross to wear around our necks. These items are useful in a personal relationship if valued and treasured.

In today's world pictures of Jesus are argued about regularly. Especially the ones that make Him look blond and European. Many Bibles go unread, and a cross around one's neck is just a piece of jewelry unless the wearing of it means something to you.

Practice makes perfect. Isn't that what our parents told us? So it is with embracing God. Let us explore this singular journey of ours, this personal relationship with the Divine, by moving forward and developing a closeness, a bond with Him. We need to practice welcoming Him into our day to day.

Religious symbols express the invisible to us by giving us a visual representation. Symbolism is used by different faiths to help us focus our devotion. The history of religious symbology is quite interesting.

Early Christians used a fish to represent Jesus Christ, the Son of God, and our Savior. This symbol is used to this day, and we often see the "Jesus Fish" on the backs of cars. The fish symbol also served as a secret sign to identify meeting places for early Christians, and the Bible references fish quite often.[7] Jesus, remember, did invite His disciples to become fishers of men.

White doves are still used to symbolize peace and purity. It was the Sign of the Dove that would identify the Messiah to John the Baptist.[8]

The Celtic cross, the cross with a circle around where the lines intersect, has a different history depending on which book one reads. The Celtic cross originated in Ireland and Scotland. Like many other symbols and Christian religious practices, this cross is thought to be the combination of religious and pagan symbology.[9]

Other religious rites that symbolize faith are the ceremonies of baptism, circumcision, confirmation, Bar Mitzvah, communion, and marriage. These practices are but a ceremony unless we attach deeper meaning and have a personal connection to them. We can use them as opportunities to celebrate with the Divine.

Should any of these symbols or rites be a part of your faith, use them with love to motivate you toward daily devotion and meditation. And let us not forget about prayer and music. I heard a quote from Rabindranath Tagore and turned it into a favorite bookmark. "God respects me when I work, but he loves me when I sing!"

As a Christian, I have explored other faiths with great respect. So many religious practices resonate with me. My religious horizons have expanded well beyond Christianity in order to bring God closer and more evident in my personal life. Where I grew up with a King James Version of the Bible,

I now have several other translations, because different renditions can offer different insight. I am especially fond of the translations from Aramaic and Greek. From my travels, I have Bibles in languages other than English. The differences are remarkable as each translator has a different gift.

Looking for new ways to ensure the Lord's presence in my life, there is a Buddha statue in my backyard, and Buddhist prayer flags flying. Buddha means "enlightened one" and seeing that Buddha reminds me of the work it takes to achieve a life of spiritual wisdom. There is a mezuzah on the door to my home. I want to take the Lord with me when I leave my home, and when I am inside of it as well. Touching that symbol reminds me of the message in it, that I should love the Lord my God with all my heart, with all my soul, and with all my strength.

I have anointing oil from Jerusalem, blessed Dead Sea salt from Israel, Holy Water from the River Jordan, and sand from a sacred Buddhist mandala.

Each in its own way helps me to commune with my Lord as often as possible during my days and nights. These items are so much more than a collection of religious items, as I use them to see Him everywhere in my home, in my backyard, in my comings and goings, and in the entirety of my life. These are some of the tools I use to supplement my Christian faith by inviting Him in at every level. They are the instruments on which I play my love for Him. My great hope would be that I might have the gift of faith.

Trust that He is always there. Our efforts to be closer to God are blessings that will be abundant as we practice. Remember, it is true that when we seek Him, we will find Him.

49

It's All a Mystery

❧☙

God. Life. Death. It is all still a mystery, isn't it? Oh, we have our thoughts, opinions, perceptions...but what do we really know? We believe our Earth was formed some four and a half billion years ago. Our ancestors arrived about six millennia back, and modern man showed up two hundred thousand years ago, give or take. And here we are!

Death. There is no escaping this fate. Scientists argue about biological immortality, but we humans are not even close to that. Yet we love to interpret and debate what happens after our hearts beat for the last time. Plenty of speculation regarding heaven, hell, and reincarnation, but nothing for sure, at least as far as indisputable proof is concerned.

Life. Yes, we have been around a couple hundred thousand years. We have had our ups and downs; civilizations have come and gone as well. The dinosaurs may be gone, but we humans are still here until the next big meteor hits, or we pollute our environment to the brink of no return. Of course, there is always the Rapture that I still hope will be the way I travel to heaven.

God. Some of us are sure of His existence. Many do not care one way or another. And then there are the ones who fight to prove He does not exist. Interesting to push so hard in the direction of non-existence, don't you think?

Here's the thing, it is all still a mystery. Two hundred thousand years of modern man with good brains, survival skills, creative proficiencies, incredible cleverness, and what have we come up with that is categorically certain about these topics?

Judaism was the first religion with a single God. Prior to that the beliefs in existence had many gods and goddesses that represented everything from weather to rituals. The God of Christianity is a trinity of three: Father, Son, and Holy Spirit. The world did not jump from Judaism into Christianity the day that the Lord Jesus was resurrected. Neither was the whole world Jewish at the time.

Christianity certainly is not now the same religion it was when it first began. There were plenty of notable spiritual, religious, and social leaders around the world prior to Jesus, any a few since Him, whether we care to acknowledge them or not. It is not unusual for Christians to assume beliefs pre-Jesus were hedonistic.

Many spiritual men, pre-Jesus were great teachers with texts and poems still read today. Some of these philosophers and prophets have countless followers still. They taught faith, love and devotion. They instructed us to abstain from hate, greed, and ignorance. They are a part of our civilization's history.

Officially, the world has thousands of religions. I have to believe that everyone else is not wrong just because they do not believe the way I do. Every preacher, every Sunday School teacher, puts his and her own perceptions and experiences into the message they share...no matter which Biblical translation they speak from. For every human has experiences from which we learn.

And perhaps that is why church membership is declining at such a rapid rate for the past several decades? Churches are now said to be culturally irrelevant. This is shocking to those of us who grew up always having a church home.

But younger generations have taken a different approach with their time and their money.

Hopefully that means people are finding more personal ways to connect to God. Finding our own spirituality may be exactly what is needed, and what is happening.

We all know our lives, culture and times have changed dramatically over the years, and maybe it is time for each of us to put more spirituality into our lives, perhaps by creating our own personal houses of worship? Perhaps it will be our first step on the singular journey we each must take down 'Relationship Road' to the true house of the Lord.

In the end, we each have to come to terms with what we believe and what we do not. Create the way you want to learn and find your place with Him. Christ will show up when you ask. Your spirituality will grow. The close, personal relationship you long for will find its home in the sanctity of that singular bond you have with Him.

Find your place to worship, the one that enriches you, and get to know Him. It may be in a church, on the Internet, or on a backyard bench. Find your faith and discover new ways to commune with the only One that really matters. Know that all things are possible through Him.

50

The Wakeup Call

୨୦ ୦୧

Good Morning – This is your wake-up call. Don't we all need one of these occasionally? Might be from a hotel operator or from a period in our lives. Maybe we hope that a friend or family member gets a wakeup call when we know they are struggling? Maybe it is a bad test score, or a job we didn't get, or one we do not enjoy? Perhaps it is a health scare for someone close to us?

A wakeup call forces us to take a closer look at what we may have been avoiding. Like refocusing the lens on our lives. I know that all I can ever offer to this life or to God is my truth. My honest self; my loving heart; putting it out there for the world. It is enough. Yet not always an easy thing to do.

In fact, this is our true purpose here on Earth: to discover our own individual humanity. As some would describe it, finding our authentic selves. That's what is left when all the façades are removed. Yes, after the designer clothes or the boots come off, the corporate and physically demanding world forgotten for the weekend. The personality that longs to surface when we find we can be without the anger or jealousy, without the selfishness or lack of self-confidence.

This is the part of life that is not a race or a competition. It is why we are here. We know this soul is there, but we often apply masks and illusions for protection because this is our most vulnerable self. One could argue, this is when we are most beautiful...

It is true that God is everywhere, and accessible always. Many of us learn about God, about Jesus. Some can quote scripture all day long. Several will argue about what God wants, what He demands of us, and where everyone is doing it wrong. It is easy to quote scripture.

Then there is knowing God. Just as accessible, and still everywhere, my God already knows me, and wants me to know Him. Knowing God is the most rewarding aspect of life. Like any relationship, wanting to bring God closer means you want to know more about Him, so you ask questions, read, and take all the answers into the deepest part of your soul. And your soul will sing with joy.

This is how we garden our souls. By sharing the joy of relationship with God. Knowing the Living God is in our minds and in our hearts will alter our lives and experiences from the inside out. We will be able to express our true selves joyfully and confidently without the need for masks and illusions.

If our lives have been fallow and we have only known about God, let our wakeup call be to get to know Him, and awaken to the joy He will bring to our lives.

51

"I Don't Know How to Love Him"

❧☙

'Jesus Christ Superstar,'[10] the 1970 rock opera was presented as a live musical telecast in 2018. This song, with the same title as this chapter, is sung by the character Mary Magdalene, about Jesus.

Many folks have no idea how to start to really love God. And it is often hard to describe what that kind of relationship with the Lord is to someone else. Words are only descriptive to a point when it comes to feelings. A beautiful sunrise can be described with colors and clouds and shadows. But love? That is all feelings and emotions so personal, it seems impossible.

A personal relationship with God is completely about love. Imagine talking about real emotional love for Jesus? Everyone has a different understanding of what is meant by love. Some may understand love as 'like' or 'adore.' We could 'feel affection for' or 'be devoted to'…or we can 'hold someone dear.' Yet each of us has different feelings about the use of those words.

My first introduction to a having a loving relationship with God came on a visit with a former high school teacher of mine. A classmate and I had stayed in touch with that teacher after we had gone off to college, and we would visit with her for weekends during the summer. Not that religion had ever come up before, but one weekend our teacher invited us to participate in a fellowship group held one evening while we were visiting.

The gathering was filled with people of all ages, and lots of music. Music popular at the time that was typically considered to be about a couple's relationship. It was opened an entirely new perspective to us.[11]

Relationship can simply be defined as the state of being connected, or the way in which two people view and behave toward each other. A friendly relationship is a strong bond that exists between people who share common values or interests. It implies a solid connection.

The deeper the relationship, the more feelings are involved. And here is an element of being human that most of us would prefer to avoid... feelings...and showing any emotion or sensitivity. Culturally these are most acceptable when not on display. Western civilization, for example, appreciates non-public displays of affection. Go ahead and have a warm and feeling heart, but do not bring it to the office or show it where others can see. Keep those tender, caring, and sympathetic feelings to yourself, if you don't mind.

But we are going to talk about just that, because those compassionate, kind, and thoughtful feelings are the center of having a personal relationship with our friends, our family, and our God.

Emotions are instinctive and intuitive in human beings. Truly a gift from God, our emotions protect us and offer us a means of expression for everything that happens in our lives. If we use them and express them, we are healthier physically, and psychologically. And we are afraid to death of them. We fear that openly manifesting them will characterize us as weak, delicate, and inadequate. We do not even realize that being vulnerable is truly a superpower.

Love. A joyous emotion experienced as a strong and happy feeling which is directed toward an object or a person. Those feelings are accompanied by biological and behavioral changes in our bodies. Love. Devotion. Tenderness. Adoration. Emotional love makes the difference in any relationship, and also with our relationship with God.

How to start that close and emotional relationship with Him?

- Meet with Him daily. Start talking to Him every day. Nothing formal, just casual chit chat. Perhaps about starting a whole new day.
- Learn more about what He promises. Read. Be open with friends. Find a place of worship. Have discussions with others. Find an advisor to trust.
- Be open and honest. He already knows all about you, but open up and talk to Him about your understanding of who you really are, and who you want to become.
- Genuine love is what will open the door to that personal loving relationship with Him. It is about trust.
- Know that the Lord, is on your side always.
- He is love, and compassion, and mercy. Open your heart to feeling the love He has for you, and you for Him. That will make all the difference.

52

Inside Out

෨෬

When do you think we first start to come up with the façade that hides our authentic selves? As a child to please a parent. As a schoolkid to gratify a teacher. As a teenager to impress a potential date. Or perhaps as an adult trying to please a society in which we are taught that our life will be great only if we follow the rules: to be a good citizen, get married at the appropriate time, have 2.5 children, and earn enough money to make at least a few others jealous. Result: Happy and fulfilled life. Done.

As we grow and mature, we try on all manner of things to see how they fit, carrying each one of those experiences in life with us. This in turn, makes us who we are today. Yet not every one of those events were happy and blissful, now were they? But they each have a memory, a feeling and a reaction. Some make our hearts sing with joy, and we delight in remembering them. Others created deep wounds and hurt with anger now standing at the ready to protect our feelings and our souls from the fear of the pain recurring.

Children, don't you think, get a pass. They need to learn right from wrong, and truth from lies. They are learning how to be in the world. Teenagers challenge everything as they must learn to spread their wings and make good decisions. But what about adults? Do we get a pass for not being who we truly are?

As humans we live inside out. We speak of our beliefs and our values, yet what we demonstrate to the world, is that façade we cover our souls with. That cover-up of hurts and subsequent fears that we have lived and learned to use to protect our vulnerability and treasured essence.

We talk a good story. We say we are Christian, or Jew; or Muslim...we say we follow God. We try to mean it, yet the struggle is real. We claim our dogma and religious texts to be our own, but we would rather argue and fight and divide our brethren, than try for compassion and unity. We ask ourselves why but refuse to believe the answer is our own fear of not being good enough, and the internal anger of not being able to think ourselves out of it.

The adage, 'actions speak louder than words' comes into play, like what we do when we think no one is looking. What we say when we assume no one is listening. Who we love is not simply who we want to love, it becomes what society wants. Are we kind or are we angry all the time? Are we embarrassed sometimes to say we have a Godly dogma we are trying to follow when we know our behavior is shameful?

Are we so angry deep inside that we throw our hate towards those who do not believe exactly the way we do about our faith? Do we hold on so tightly to what we are supposed to believe that we have never taken the time to see if we are, truly in our hearts, believing what we say out loud?

Letting our true loving selves out into the open takes some effort. One needs to take all the love we long to feel and apply it to every aspect of our lives and our world. That is the challenge. But we need to heal that disguise we have created deep inside. We must not only feel the love of God, but also show it by believing that all people are doing their very best. This is not always easy. But think about that for a moment or two. If that is something we can truly believe, we can move forward with a more loving perspective.

We must believe that those who have hurt us, lashed out only because they were hurting and angry first. If we share and give love, forgiveness will follow. Forgiveness for ourselves, and for all those people who hurt us. It is so important to express our love genuinely and emotionally. Human emotion is a gift from God that we should learn to appreciate and express, as we must also learn to accept and feel the love from the God we have put our faith in. It is in the emotion of feeling love that love can heal us.

Until our first reaction to all circumstances is love, compassion and blessing to whatever is going on, we still have work to do on ourselves. It all starts with accepting the fact that our cover-up is just that. It is our protective armor, and we do not need it any longer. When we feel and share love we will find what we need for our true selves to finally emerge.

Acceptance of ourselves and others breeds compassion. Compassion breeds kindness, and kindness...well, that ought to be a conviction we all share.

53

Bible Stories

☙❧

The Bible is often called the 'Book of Books,' because it contains not only historical information, but also rules for us to live by, some parables and prophecy, and at the same time, literature. The Bible speaks of the special relationship of God and His chosen people. It speaks of faith, salvation, and the problem of evil. But there is not just one Bible.

There has always been a challenge to understand why different Christian faiths have varying numbers of books in the Bible. The Protestant Bible has 66 books: Old Testament 39, and New Testament 27. But the Old Testament in the Catholic Bible contains 46 books, and if one is of the Eastern or Oriental Orthodox faiths, that Old Testament may contain up to 51 books. There is great variety to the number of words contained in the Bible as well.

And then there are Bible languages. The Old Testament was first written in an ancient form of Hebrew. The writings that became the New Testament are believed to have been written some 400 years later. The New Testament writings were in a combination of Aramaic, Koine Greek (an ancient Greek no longer spoken), and a colloquial dialect of Mishnaic Hebrew.

The English language alone has hundreds of translations of the Bible available. From original transcriptions, the Bible was translated from ancient languages into Greek. Then a Pope Damascus I, had the Bible translated into Latin.

The most famous and 'authorized version' of the Bible is the King James Version. That was created by forty-seven scholars, each a member of the Church of England. Begun in 1604, this English version was created specifically for the Church of England, and was commissioned by King James I. It took about seven years to complete.

Meant with no disrespect, thousands of scholars have taken a hand at translating the Bible, and still do to this day. Some are better at Greek than Hebrew; others better at Latin. Interesting things can happen when words are translated, and words from one language do not always translate easily into another.

Even if we do not participate in religion, we all quote the Bible in our everyday language. Examples: "Salt of the earth" or "fight the good fight" or "the powers that be" are all taken directly from the Bible.

The Bible is quoted as often by those who support war, as those who support peace. It has been used to both promote and discredit slavery. The Bible makes people rejoice, and it makes people very angry. It is a book that is revered as well as spurned. The Bible has inspired artists, scholars, and a legion of faithful congregants. Artists from multiple centuries have been inspired to depict Biblical stories.

Ever wonder how to dispose of a Bible? There is no definite, agreed upon method.

The more we read it, the more we learn that Biblical stories are often not quite what they seem to be. We have familiarity with a few stories, but should we add in the surrounding verses, the theme may well change. We tend to pick and choose what we want to share from the Bible and ignore the parts that do not support our opinions.

We need to learn to take in the Bible as a whole. It is a tough read without a doubt, and graphic too, and it is not all fairytales and parables. It is about life then and now. It is about love and forgiveness, and compassion. It is about hate and evil, and everlasting life. The Bible is about praying in secret, and not making a public display of it. It is about many incredible stories beyond the scope of Sunday school. Maybe it is time for us to start digging into it a bit and discovering the real stories it holds.

Seek out different translations of this Good Book and find the ones that resonate with you and your heart. The Bible can come alive in a whole different way.

And speaking about Bible translations and stories and praying, I want to share with you my very favorite version of the Lord's Prayer translated by Mark Hathaway into English directly from the ancient Aramaic language:

"O Cosmic Birther of all radiance and vibration!

Soften the ground of our being and carve out a space within us where your Presence can abide.

Fill us with your creativity so that we may be empowered to hear the fruit of our mission.

Let each of our actions bear fruit in accordance with our desire.

Endow us with the wisdom to produce and share what each being needs to grow and flourish.

Untie the tangled threads of destiny that bind us, as we release from the entanglement of past mistakes.

Do not let us be seduced by that which would divert us from our true purpose, but illuminate the opportunities of the present moment.

For you are the ground and the fruitful vision, the power and the fulfillment, as all is gathered and made whole once again."[12]

54

"Some Things are True...

❧☙

"Whether you believe them or not." A quote from the character, Seth, in the 1998 movie, City of Angels. Now that is a quote I have used on more than one person since hearing it. Of course, you do not have to believe me...

Each of our lives is completely individualized. Despite being in the same family, each member has a different perspective, a unique life experience here on Earth. Every human's experience is filtered through individual upbringing, our unique sensibilities, or lack thereof, and our personal interpretation of events. Hard to believe? Ask your siblings to describe their childhood and parents and see how closely their descriptions match yours. Of course, as an only child, there can be only one way to describe my childhood...

Individual. Unique. Distinct. Original. That's us. And it is what often makes truth so hard to come by. Imagine two, ten, or a hundred people describing an incident. Each story varies. Each impact on that human being inimitable. We each enjoy a unique singular journey through life.

Honestly, I struggle with the fact that dinosaurs existed. I have seen skeletal remains and all. I have seen the fossils.

And yet I still find it unimaginable that those amazing creatures walked where I walk today.

I am okay though with Moses parting the Red Sea, and Jonah sitting in that big whale for three days. No issue either with Daniel surviving the lion's den, or the Immaculate Conception. I have no difficulty with Jesus turning water into the finest wine, or Him walking on water. And forty years of manna from heaven? Yeah, totally doable. Feeding the masses with a few loaves of bread and some fish? Yep, I am definitely on board.

Healing the blind and the deaf...raising the dead... curing lepers and paralytics...I have no problem with miracles.

It often seems miraculous we can agree on anything. And yet if we combine our individual experiences with the diversity of our personalities, we still find ways to create community and neighborhoods, and countries, which is really something remarkable. We even find ways to procreate. So, we must all get along sometime.

As humans we need to feel that we belong and are accepted. We find ways to gather and to get along. We join organizations and give charitably. However, along with that tribal instinct to belong, we also use the kinship we feel with different groups to feel superior and right in opposing people whose ideas are different from our own, whose truths are dissimilar. We seek to take advantage of others because of the power we long to feel. We love to feel. We desire control because it feels awesome.

Control feels amazing because it gives us a deep sense of security and of certainty. If we can control our environment, we will survive what we are facing.

But today, when many of us have food and sleep and shelter, the dangers are very different from those of our ancestors. However, our instincts still play a role. And in this world, we still can feel out of control with politicians causing us to feel unsafe from other countries, or our neighbors' secretly taking prescription drugs and not behaving normally. Perhaps our friends are suffering from divorce or health issues. It is not an easy task to find the power within.

What is important is to look for that power. We are each born with an amazing power within ourselves, and we are not all aware of that. That is our authentic power. That place inside ourselves that can guide us to our own truth. There is something else there. The kingdom of God is within us.

What can help to bring us to that place within ourselves is faith. The same faith that allows our minds and hearts to trust in fantastic Bible stories and have confidence that inside of us is a strength beyond our current comprehension.

And once we build that faith to be strong and unshakable, we will learn to live that faith with more than a thankful heart. For we will allow that faith, that love, to change who we are. We will demonstrate our faith in our words and in our deeds. And those actions will be performed in the name of the Lord. Amen.

55

The Greatest Illusionist

☙❧

We think of illusionists as magicians...prestidigitators... conjurers. Yet we humans are the greatest at taking molecules and radiation, mixing them up with our five senses and our brains spew out virtual reality that we live our lives in. That is incredible magic if you ask me. Our minds dictate what we see in our world, and how we see it. Is it any wonder we hear that life is an illusion?

Guess what else our brains do? They take all of the people we have ever met, every book and article that we have read, any place we have lived, and each and every experience we have been through, and use those as the filters through which we view our world...our friends...our enemies...everything. Anais Nin is credited with saying, "We don't see the world as it is. We see it as we are."

Ask anyone what he or she might want out of life. The answers might be something like money, happiness, peace, a house. Ask them what gets in the way. Interestingly, it is money, but also pain, the chaos of the world, etc. What kind of focus gets us to a place where we want peace, and love and harmony, but instead we see turmoil, and suffering, and chaos?

The answer just might be that we focus on the illusion

of it all. I am sure we all understand the misconception that money buys happiness, or that impressing others with possessions means something. Why don't we put money to a quick test? If we had $50 million and were alone on a desert island, would that get us anything or anywhere? Nope, that doesn't pass the sniff test.

Let us take any ordinary day in our life. The way our day goes, will more than likely be determined by which side of the bed we got up on. Wrong side? The morning may not be the cheeriest we have experienced in our life, and the day could easily get worse. Little things may feel enormous in size and tough to get over. Get up on the right side, and we simply start our day with a smile and a happier outlook. We will probably be more forgiving of little nuisances along the way.

How does that work? Who is in control here anyway? Does each day come with a different set of rules or what? For that matter, who makes the rules?

Say it with me: 'I do. I make the rules for my life and for how my every day will play out. I can change the rules at any time, depending on how I choose to see the world.'

There have been many teachers in the world that have shown us how to change the lens through which we see and experience life. God has given each of us the talent and the ability, as well as the resources to achieve endless fulfillment in this life of ours.

Since we make our own rules, we need to learn about the consequences of each choice. Should we choose to live in the chaos, for example, in finding others to blame for our circumstances in life, we then give up the choice to make our lives really gratifying. Should we believe that to find harmony, love, and peace in our lives, we must see the world filled with these things each and every day, we open ourselves up to live lives of endless fulfillment.

If we believe in the common good, then we see that happening first.

If we come from a place of compassion, then we offer that first.

If we are willing to forgive, we can rise above that which needs forgiveness.

We need faith and confidence in ourselves and our own ability to nourish the good that we have planted inside ourselves. We must plant the seeds of love, of compassion, and forgiveness. We must exercise those abilities with every breath and with every thought. And if we catch ourselves falling back into the chaos, we must forgive ourselves and move forward.

We set the rules for the filters we use to experience our lives. If we are willing to take a risk and use this opportunity to believe for example, that our own intuition is stronger than our five senses, we then delve into the marvelous mysteries of life. If we choose God and His love, He becomes part of our filter. He is then the lens that opens the world for us to new and greater possibilities. If we choose negativity instead, we get just that.

It is essential that we accept the challenge to choose our current beliefs when better information comes along, and not fight to the death when one of our beliefs is challenged. Part of the mystery is what happens to us when we are open to the possibility of change.

We can create the illusion but must thoroughly believe in it down to the very core of our being. These are just more of God's great gifts. The free will to live a life filled with His blessings or not.

The choice, as always, is ours. If we choose the mystery, we can learn to feel safe in it, and endeavor to fill it up with endless serenity and joy.

Praying that you choose the mystery...

56

Sabbath

෨෫

Sabbath, the seventh day of the week, as first mentioned in Genesis, is supposed to be a day of rest and a day that God made holy. After all, He put it in the Ten Commandments that were given to Moses. The Sabbath is regarded by most as a perpetual covenant with God to be kept always, at least as far as Mosaic Law is concerned. It is not only a symbol of the day after the six days of creation, but also in remembrance of the Israelites deliverance from Egypt.

One day of the week, simple, right? Well, not so fast. Even when presented with the historical facts of something as simple as a day of the week, one must wonder what we are really supposed to believe. Add in the consideration of wondering what God may want, the choice gets even more confusing, and yes, we are still talking about just one day. Or are we?

The Sabbath is the seventh day of the week per the book of Exodus. But some Christians today understand the Sabbath to be a Saturday, and to others Sabbath is a Sunday. So begins the confusion of which day is the Lord's Day.

This Biblical Sabbath is filled with even more controversy. The Hebrew Sabbath begins Friday at sunset, and of course the exact time for that changes every week. It lasts until Saturday's sunset. Early Christians used the Saturday Sabbath, but by the second century AD, many had moved worship and rest to the next day, Sunday, if only to differentiate themselves from the Jews.

A few reasons exist for that change. First, the new Christianity arising after the resurrection, believed that the old laws no longer applied, as they had a new covenant with God to take their place. Others believed that because Jesus's resurrection took place on a Sunday, it created the Lord's Day, automatically making Sunday a holy day. Some other groups celebrated the Sabbath on Saturday, and the Lord's Day on Sunday with separate services.

More than a century before Christianity, Egyptian Mithraists brought about the festival of Sun-day, designed to be the day for sun worshippers to do their thing. This was just one of many pagan customs that were incorporated into the religion of the day to attract non-Christians.

Two other contributions to the move of Sabbath to Sunday came along in the early three hundreds AD. Roman Emperor Constantine worshipped the Sun god. His edict proclaiming Sun-day as a day of rest was probably an attempt to influence the populace of growing Christianity. Interesting though that after his edict, Constantine proclaimed himself a bishop of the Catholic Church.

There was also the Council of Laodicea during which sixty canons were created. A Biblical Canon is a set of books regarded by their creators as authoritative scripture. This council of Catholic clerics managed to change religious history by determining what would be a canon and therefore, what would be in the Catholic Bible. That meant what or would not be read and taught in church. This canon specifically outlaws the keeping of the Sabbath on Saturday.

And here we are some two thousand years later with some denominations still celebrating Sabbath on Saturday, and others on Sunday. What have we achieved?

Bottom line, these stories are a part of our history. The truth is important to know since we all should want to understand our faith and its beliefs, its values, and where they originated. Many hands created Bible stories, and many more decided on which books belonged in the various Bibles and which did not. We each must decide how and when to worship, what tools to use, and whether to worship individually or communally.

The bigger question may be how do we set aside a day for the Lord nowadays? How do we keep it holy? Perhaps here is where we draw on the gift of free will we were all blessed with? We can choose to follow Mosaic Law for any number of reasons or lean towards a Sunday celebration of Him. As in the old days there are many folks today who use both days on the weekend to celebrate the Lord by resting physically and mentally, as well as incorporating scripture and worship; believing in the Old Testament Sabbath as much as Sunday's Day of the Lord.

Perhaps begin by dedicating a day to Him. Keep it holy by setting that day apart from the rest of the week because upon rising you dedicate the day to Him. Consider Him in your thoughts and in your actions that day. Be thankful for this glorious life we are given. Live in grace. Share your blessings. You may find that one holy day a week is just not enough...

57

I Want Kindness

※☆※

To be my religion... Heck, I want it to be everybody's. How tired are we of the news stories coming out of our world today? The hate is overflowing: The lack of tolerance astounding. Every thought needs to be broadcast, every meal photographed, and every opinion spewed. There is no such thing as shame anymore. We embarrass ourselves as we strive to humiliate and disgrace others.

What is so sad is that anger and hate, when expressed, actually make us feel good. We feel relief to get them out. We are emoting what is trapped inside of us that desperately needs expression. However, there is a more profound underlying truth. That we are not taught about how our very human emotions work, and the need we have to express them for our own good health. In the process we repress the painful emotions such as guilt, sadness and fear, and allow them to build up inside of us. And because those feelings are buried, and unexpressed, they stay shielded by the rage and loathing that stand at the ready to explode out of us almost uncontrollably. Social media fits the bill beautifully because it gives everyone the voice they so desperately seek to express that anger, as do street protests that are riddled with violence.

Soul gardening cannot take away the rage, as that disappearing from our emotional repertoire is dependent on our own personal growth. What we can do is advocate kindness as a religion. Somehow, I do not think God would mind a little kindness in this world.

What is religion anyway? It is defined as faith and belief. Religion is the ultimate pursuit of something, a creed if you will. A formula for belief. So what if we believed that we should all be kind?

What is religion to you now? Seems humans through the centuries have made religion really very complicated. So many rights and wrongs. So many different conflicting stories. The ask here is not to change what we may believe or not believe, but to add kindness to the mix. Was that ever something mentioned in the religion you were taught or now practice? I am fairly sure everyone's mother mentioned how important it is to be kind to others...

Would we argue as much? Would we battle to see who could be more kind? Oh please, could we try that? Perhaps we would lose the viciousness on display daily in our world? It now seems we will fight to the death over just about anything. Parents get into yelling matches and full-blown fights at their children's sporting events. People won't volunteer to be referees or umpires anymore due to the insults and arguments. What are the children learning here? To be kind? To play fair? Let us not kid ourselves.

Road rage has become deadly, and politics has split friendships and families apart. We have lost more than kindness; we have lost decency. Where please is civility, decorum, or graciousness?

Blame stress. Blame others. Nothing will do any good until we get a grip on ourselves. Start here, in our own hearts and in our own minds. We have lost touch with our true selves. The soul in us that understands that hate is not the answer. The part that empathizes with others, and situations, and understands consequences. Working together is what we need so desperately to find again.

Working to persuade another is different than coming to blows. Do we really want the physically stronger to win each battle? Are we all still in junior high?

Remember what your momma taught you, what you learned if you grew up with siblings, or what was communicated to you when you first went to kindergarten. Be kind and share. Understanding that each person is different, but also that we are ultimately the same. Recognizing that multiple ideas from different sources make a greater whole. Fathoming the idea that your opinion is just great, but really doesn't need to be crammed down the throat of another.

Be gracious. Be kind. Be blessed.

58

Horatio

☙❧

Systematic investigation is not my profession, yet I do enjoy researching things that are of interest to me especially about faith and God. In this 21st century we are blessed with being able to study archaeological information hidden for centuries until very recently in many cases. The exploration can take one far and wide, and the depth and breadth of the knowledge currently available is outrageously large. It makes the investigation of information extremely difficult because there is so much volume to it all. Add to it all the interpretations made along the way, and it feels impossible to be able to learn the complete truth about anything.

    Should we do our reading or research in any modern language, we suffer from not only the language abilities of the translators, but also the philosophical perspective they held at the time. The conclusion of a Christian researcher will be biased as compared to that of the atheist researcher. Even if the scholar claims to work strictly to determine historical facts, one's internal predisposition will play a role in any translations or conclusions made. We will often not know the bias. We can just do our best to put our own intelligent reasoning into our interpretations. This is our challenge with that which is written and shared with the world. And there are so many mysteries yet to be unraveled.

Two of the things that fascinate me most are mysticism and miracles as related to faith. Jewish, Christian and Islamic religions claim that mysticism is a part of their faiths. Mysticism is a word derived from the Greek word 'to conceal' and is often applied to those parts of life that as humans we just do not understand, or perhaps those parts of living and dying that we fear.

Let us look at the Kabbalah, the ancient Jewish mystical interpretation of the Bible. Said to be given by God to Abraham, the secrets to the Kabbalah have only been revealed in the past few hundred years. The Kabbalah is supposed to provide man with wisdom to improve our lives and aid us in finding our purpose. Yet for most of the past twenty–six hundred years it has been reserved for the rabbinical community only.

We are probably most familiar with mysticism being associated with Buddhism, yoga, and Eastern traditions, but there is Christian mysticism as well. Many poopoo the idea of Christian mysticism citing that there is no such thing in Christianity today...that God is accessible to all, because that is His promise to us. He reveals Himself to us and there are no secrets involved in Christianity. Yet others believe that Christian mysticism means the development of mystical practices and theory. Roman Catholic and Orthodox Christianity admit to mystical traditions within their faiths.

Christian mysticism can be described as personal transformation through a religious experience or as a loving personal experience with God. Nonetheless, there are some who readily believe that Christianity has a mystical history reaching back to the New Testament. There have been many mystics through the centuries. It is a fascinating subject filled with rituals, mystical and contemplative prayer, visions and ecstasies.

Let us look at miracles. Did you know that many think that only Christian's believe in or should experience miracles? Nonetheless, there are other religions besides Christianity that have miracles as a part of their faith: Shamanism, Buddhism, and Taoism for example.

Depending on who one talks to, miracles happen each and every day in our lives. Now some are much larger than others and have had movies made about them. Other miracles are smaller and may be intensely personal. But any miracle, any unexplainable event is usually welcome.

Those with religious inclination know of the spectacular Biblical miracles. Many miracles that we hear about today have to do with incredible healings, improbable rescues, folks coming back to life after long periods without a heartbeat, and one recently about a wedding ring deflecting a bullet. They are each valuable tools in confirming our faith.

We seek the invisible God and look for signs that He is here with us. Both mysticism and miracles aid us in feeling the welcome presence of God. Still, though surrounded by His creations, and feeling His presence, we want more... and we know it is out there. Even Hamlet knew it when he spoke to his trusted friend and confidant...

"There are more things in heaven and earth, Horatio,
Than are dreamt of in your philosophy."
- *Hamlet* **(Act 1 Scene 5. Lines 167-8), Hamlet to Horatio**

William Shakespeare, 1601

59

"For God So Loved the World"

෨෦

You know how it goes from there, right? For God so loved the world, that he gave his only begotten Son, that whosoever believeth in him should not perish, but have everlasting life. *(John 3:16 KJV)* Our history lessons take us back hundreds of thousands of years for the creation of our Universe, yet our religious training takes us back only about two thousand years or so. That was, we are told, when our Jesus was born.

Most of the time, we humans have trouble looking at the big picture of life on this planet. But we are taught that way in schools. Memorize when this war happened and the year that this document was signed. As we learn to live our lives, we find ourselves so wrapped up in our own personal trials and tribulations that we feel the need to focus only on the here and now. For example, we of think Jesus, but we do not put Him into the perspective of all the peoples who came before, what was going on at the time from any other perspective, let alone all the other humans who have walked the planet. We do not even realize that in the title saying, "for God so loved the world" at that moment, that it makes it sound like God did not start to love us until He decided to send us our Yeshua!! (Yeshua is Hebrew for Jesus.) I don't believe that is true.

Since my faith encompasses love of God and life in general, I have to believe that God loved us and all of existence since the beginning of time. After all, God created all that we see, all that we have, and all of the unseen Universe as well. That being the case I would propose that God's love transcended the millennia to give us many other people prior to Jesus, and some after Him as well, to help us cope with this singular journey called life. I am just suggesting that God's love gave us more than one life to have respect for, and perhaps we can also benefit from the perspectives that others gave to our world.

We will skip over Moses and Abraham, as we have familiarity with them since they are part of the Old Testament. Without any prejudice, let us first look at Krishna, one of the earliest compassionate religious persons we know to exist.

Three thousand years BC Krishna was born into a Hindu family. As a supreme god to the Hindus, Krishna taught about compassion, tenderness, and love. He spoke of the war between good and evil in humankind, and of the nature of true peace. That is five thousand years ago folks. Krishna is known for the Hindu scripture known as the Bhagavad Gita, which literally translated means "The Song of God."[13]

Zoroaster, also known as Zarathustra, was born about three thousand years ago. As an ethical philosopher, Zoroaster taught spiritual philosophy. His teaching included a belief in heaven and hell, judgment after death, and free will. He believed in a single supreme being and of our struggles with good and evil. Zoroastrianism is still practiced today.[14]

Confucius, the Chinese philosopher, teacher, and politician, was born five hundred years BC. His philosophies focused on morality, honesty, and integrity. Confucianism is still alive today, mostly in China.[15]

Siddhartha Gautama, also known as the Buddha, was born about the same time as Confucius. The Four Noble Truths which are the foundation of Buddhism, was the Buddha's first sermon after his Enlightenment. He was an enlightened individual, meaning he became spiritually aware. Buddhism, whose goal is to overcome suffering and the human cycle of death and rebirth, is currently the world's fourth largest religion.[16]

Socrates lived centuries before Christ. Truth was what Socrates loved. He believed that man walked a sacred path of love for philosophy and wisdom. He also believed in the reincarnation of an eternal soul. One of his most famous quotes is that "an unexamined life is not worth living." Socrates was sentenced to death for corrupting young people with his philosophies. Socrates taught Plato, who then taught Aristotle. What philosophical gifts they each brought us.[17]

Sacred texts from many of the above are still being read today...as history, as philosophy, and as a way of life. Do not forget that religion is also a way of life. I see all these men with all their writings and philosophies as blessings that we can still read about and live by today. Perhaps a different perspective from our Jesus, yet perhaps much of the same. We are still talking, and working towards a more compassionate, tender, loving way to live.

Consider the Baha'i teachings that God is revealed throughout history by persons who are Manifestations of God. Those who are born to found the major religions of the world...like Krishna, Buddha, and Jesus. Prophets who unify us with love and acceptance by bringing their divine attributes to humankind, therefore allowing us to feel closer to God.[18]

Just a thought as I look at the world and consider the possibilities. Imagine the idea that God has been expressing Himself throughout our entire history by sending us His messengers along the way!

60

Spiritual Anxiety

The apprehension can start at most any time. It can even begin early in childhood when a church tells a child that one of his parents will go to hell because that parent is not of a particular religion. The worry can spring up in a young person when she tells lies that she's told is a sin to do. Perhaps the young adult's unease rises from the sin of sex, or even the thought of sex. This nervousness and angst starts in many of us very early on, and it does not really get better with age.

For many decades politics and religion have been taboo topics in most social settings. This of course is pre-social media. The disquiet is out in the open now, but that does not solve anything, it has just made it okay to admit one feels anxious. We should have discussed those topics all along so we could have learned how to appreciate rather than denigrate another's differing opinion.

Not sure if you have noticed, but we are taught the same Bible stories over and over. There are societal lessons to be learned from those tales, and the truth is, it does seem we need to hear them over and over because they go in one ear and out the other. We do not take them in, contemplate them, and put the morals to good use.

We are more comfortable clinging to those basic stories, and we would prefer not to be challenged by any new information that is revealed. Whether or not new information is true, is another story, but we are challenged by new theories regularly. Examples that come to mind are *The Bible Code*,[19] the *Gospel of Judas*,[20] or the concept that Mary and Jesus were husband and wife.

Now the *Bible Code* told us that if one compiled various letters of the Torah in Hebrew, that all the world's greatest events were spelled out as if in a secret code written thousands of years ago.

In the *Gospel of Judas*, we are told that Judas did not betray Jesus, but that Jesus asked Judas to turn Him over to the authorities.

The theory about Mary and Jesus being married was speculated because rabbis were typically married in those times. There have also been interpretations made of the painting of the Last Supper by Leonardo da Vinci.

Did any of these catch you off guard? Did you feel betrayed? Were you shaken? Perhaps you vehemently argued for what you believed is true?

Personally, I loved the *Bible Code* tales. And what Judas did or did not do, did not shake my faith, nor did the husband/wife thing. But I know many who were deeply affected by these supposed revelations. They each brought a level of anxiety to many faithful, who did not know how to handle it.

There is another type of spiritual anxiety. The one we find while we are on a deeper spiritual path. Opening to all that God has to offer us is like following a calling. As we seek understanding, the door is opened to us to unveil what has been clouding our perceptions. Apprehensiveness can soon follow.

Apparently, this anxiousness is fairly common, and it can be described as spiritual depression or even the dark night of the soul. It comes from spiritual distress and invokes a disruption in one's belief system. Our belief system is the basis for the way we live our lives. It is a painful feeling of alienation when there is a disturbance in one's life principles.

It can happen while we are on this singular journey toward union with God. This has been written about over and over across the centuries. One of the most famous poems about this is written by Saint John of the Cross, a Spanish mystic and a figure of the counter-reformation. The poem is called 'Dark Night of the Soul.'

What one experiences during this dark night of the soul may include anger or fear, or even a loss of hope. Keep seeking guidance from Him as you seek this deeper knowing and understanding of God. Remember you are on a path of the purest love. Once the dark night is over, the soul garners a more profound perception and appreciation for all that is.

It is in the deeper perceptions and feelings that we learn that our faith cannot be shaken. That anxiety will not overtake us, because our very core is bathed in love and understanding.

61

Shift Happens

I was brought up to believe that the battle between Good and Evil was very real, and ever present in our lives. As humans it is our choice of how to live each day. It is Right vs. Wrong. God vs. Satan. Period.

Now I do understand that this Right and Wrong methodology is the only way to grow a human. How else could we teach children what they should and should not be doing? We cannot expect a child to understand 'sometimes' let alone 'on occasion.' We have to teach them 'always' and 'never' for quite a few years.

Growing into adulthood we find that a very wide gray area exists everywhere. It is that gap in between the pure black and the pure white that most of us live in most of the time. If we ever learned about God vs. Satan, we have long forgotten that in favor of what we consciously see, and subconsciously fear. The thought that Good vs. Evil is at the root of everything may be there deep down inside of us somewhere. But the possible reality of that being true is too much to deal with on a daily basis.

Right and Wrong plays into the shift. If we believe someone did something 'wrong,' we do not have much sympathy for them. After all, we each have choices to make, right? If we believe people are doing things 'right,' or behaving correctly, we tend to look upon the person with a more compassionate eye. How much we may or may not love the person involved may well take a back seat to our perception of the 'right' or 'wrong' opinion.

What is the shift? It is when we take a giant leap forward in our own enlightenment and stop being so judgmental with everything. This disparaging behavior is fall out from our 'right' vs. 'wrong' childhood environment. We unconsciously label our lives with 'good' and 'bad' and it flings us into automatic pejorative behavior.

We also tend to lose sight of just having an opinion about things, and rush completely to judgment. We are surrounded by people who are looking for someone else to blame for whatever they conceive to be wrong in their lives or in the world. We do this and we know it is true, and we need to knock it off. This is hindering our growth as humans, let alone as spiritual beings. Back out of that judgment and allow yourself to simply have an informed opinion. Let us not rush to judgment at the first whiff of impropriety. An opinion can mean having a very strong view of something, yet allowing that there is the possibility that there may be more facts we are unaware of. Or we might just be wrong. Being judgmental means we have already reached an unyielding conclusion.

Our greatest challenge, however, is to stop criticizing and judging ourselves. We each do it to one degree or another. This is a very serious affliction that we bear. We punish ourselves with words of disgust and shame. We blame our parents as well as our upbringing for who we are, and never take responsibility that our actions are our own. And we are never going to lose the judging of others until we can recover from doing it to ourselves.

There is a well-known quote about people doing the very best they can at any moment. I wonder if you believe that of yourself. Could you try? That alone can and will open the door to the possibility of empathy and acceptance on a wider scale than one has experienced before. How about this possibility: That we are equal in the eyes of God?

For the sake of our own enlightenment, we must try to understand the person or the situation we are judging. Ourselves included. Learn to accept others as they are... God's children. The same as we are. We need to learn to awaken our understanding of the way life works, by showing love and compassion. It will not cost us a dime. But we may just learn that love transcends suffering. What a beautiful lesson that would be to learn.

Now that would create a shift, would it not? Shift does happen! When we shift our thinking, we change our lives.

62

What's In a Name?

ಸಿಂ ಡಿ

Often the gift of generations past, our names are a precious gift bestowed with love. Parents can spend endless hours trying to decide what their bundle of joy should be called. Shall we follow what our families have done for generations past? Or should we wander in the direction of a more modern name? Perhaps you are named after a well-loved relative? I was. Maybe you are a junior? You name will be on your diplomas, your degrees, and your gravestone. You name is how you will be remembered by your family, by your friends, and by all those you spend time with in your life. You name will convey the reputation you have built using it.

Names individualize us. We are unique, different, and special. Yet it seems in this great big world we have built; it is not enough to just remember each distinctive person with his or her own name and attributes. Somewhere along the line we humans felt the need to use labels to categorize each other. We created stereotypes and tags that describe people and groups, usually symbolizing incredible negativity.

I guess humans have always struggled with acceptance, for with that struggle comes the need to separate from those traits that we do not understand. Attributes we choose not to appreciate. Characteristics that we fear. Qualities that we are jealous of, and mannerisms of the groups we long to be a part of, or that we do not want to be associated with.

When we label others, not only do we do a disservice to them, we do damage to ourselves and to our good name. Justice may be blind, but we are not. We formulate immediate conclusions when we meet people. Not only do we assign gender, race, weight, and sexual orientation distinctions to each, but we also believe we know exactly how that person lives, feels, and votes based on our conclusions.

We ignorantly believe that sex equals gender. We think skin color and dialect designates not only where a person might be from, but perhaps what a person is likely to believe and support. We assign qualities like laziness and lack of intelligence to people who weigh too much for our tastes. Hair styles and personal attributes often point us towards deciding sexual orientation. The way someone chooses to dress themselves, gives us an impression of their income level, and the way they speak, their education level.

And if we get to know someone a little bit and find out what their interests might be, or their religion? Forget about it. We are ready to label those characteristics as well.

The labeling is so common, we do not even realize the consequences of our thoughts. We are lumping people together in a derogatory way. Stereotyping is not a positive action. Instead it is an assumed behavior that we think everyone in a particular group participates in doing.

Does any part of that sound compassionate? It certainly does not sound like a reality most of us would want to be a part of. It is a means of blatant and unconscious prejudice where we pigeonhole the rest of the world to make ourselves feel better and to deem ourselves superior.

Let us have this be a call to action for us all. Let us stop assigning labels that blame and condemn others who are wonderfully different from us. May we meet new people with an openness to the beautiful complexity of the human spirit. May we learn to be colorblind to skin color. May we accept personal, religious, and political differences and move on. Let our names represent our true selves in the goodness we show to others.

The Golden Rule says that we should do unto others as we would want them to do unto us. Did you know that there exists variations of the Golden Rule in dozens of religions?

Though we label others, not one of us wants to be labeled. We want to be the individuals our names allow us to be. We long to be taken as the unique soul we are in this life. Let us give others the same gift.

63

Knock, Knock

❧☙

Who's there? God. God who? Could that be the problem? That we do not know God, at least the way He would like us to know Him.

Do you want to know God, or just know about Him? Perhaps your answer is: What's the difference? Or perhaps it is what is in it for me, either way? Or maybe though you have heard of God, you are just not sure of what you believe. Perchance you have heard of Him and once believed, but now you are angry.

Any answer is just fine. Think about it though, essentially God can be like a person your friends tell you about, but you have never met. That is knowing about someone. They exist. Even if that someone is God. Knowing God is similar to how you know your closest friends. You are comfortable in their presence. You like to hang out with them, and most of the time, you know exactly how they will react in different circumstances.

So, what is the big deal? God being an integral part of one's life is a choice only you can make and act on. This one choice can change your life, and all your experiences with it. This one selection can change your heart and your mind. It can alter the direction that life takes, as well as bring a peace to your being that others, unfamiliar with Him, cannot understand. It simply does depend on what you want from this precious life.

Chances are good you are looking for ways to better understand and communicate with the Divine. Based on that, let us look at some of the many promises that God makes to those of us who believe in Him.

We are told that if we delight in the Lord, He will give us the desires of our hearts. He tells us we need not be anxious about anything, but that in every situation we should present our requests to God, and the peace of God will guard our hearts and our minds.

It all sounds so easy and complicated at the same time. The desires of our hearts? Does that mean our material desires? Or our authentic heart's desires? Really, don't be anxious? In this century? Everything makes us anxious, especially if we watch the news.

As usual, we need to take a step back from the day to day turmoil. The state of the world. The anxiety of everyday life. We need to look at the truth of who we really are deep down inside, and what would truly fulfill us as human beings. This is all part of recovering our authentic selves. That innate part of us that is pure and loving and peaceful. All that other negativity is what we learn as we grow up and are forced to cope with other's hatred and greed. Our souls suffer at the hands of others who are angry and disenchanted from not getting what they feel they want and deserve out of life.

Longing for peace in this world. Searching for loving kindness in the everyday. Making this life a more joyful experience. That is what I think we all ultimately want to have and to share with the world. Many of us look for these in religion. Most religions teach some sort of meditation or introspection or prayer. But do we just recite what we are given as examples of how to pray? Is there any other guidance we can use?

The Lord tells us to ask, to seek, and to knock. If we ask

it will be given; if we seek, we will find; and if we knock, the door will be opened unto us.

In prayer or meditation, invite Him to come into your life and guide it always. Summon His protection and forgiveness. Request to find peace in every aspect of your life. Use your words to open your heart to Him. Find the lyrics to "What a Friend We Have in Jesus" and sing it like you mean it.

Seek His counsel and His guidance in every aspect of your life. Find opportunities to be more compassionate. Strive to feel His abiding love. Just because we have heard that God loves us, it is not the same as us feeling loved. We must use our minds and hearts to try to comprehend and experience all that this loving God has to offer His children. Pursue ways to learn about Him and grow closer to Him by cultivating any relationship.

Knock on the door to God's complete acceptance and love. Be welcomed into His loving arms. There is peace there, and the comfort we all need.

As you receive God's blessings, share them with others. Learn empathy, mercy, and grace. Practice loving kindness, forgiveness, and compassion. Become a conduit for God's love, and you will feel and know His blessing.

64

Repeat After Me

☙❧

Remember learning the times tables or tackling a new language? Perhaps you learned to play an instrument and was told to practice daily? How many times did folks tell you that practice makes perfect? If you tried to practice just once a week, not much progress would be made. But every day? Wow. That kicked the learning into high gear. It is magical to watch and feel that burst of learning happening with the numbers, and the words, and the notes suddenly beginning to flow.

That same theory applies no matter what we are trying to understand and learn: schoolwork, job skills, and sports. All of it. So, why do we typically have worship services only once a week? And today, with western civilization the active 24/7 it is, how many of us even make that service a requirement for our lives?

Should we attend such services, even on the Holidays, it feels as easy as riding a bicycle. We remember the liturgies, the hymns, and the need to bring a few bucks for the offering plate. We know the timing of what happens when. The Lord's Prayer, memorized as a child, rolls off the tongue as easy as seeing a friend and asking how they are doing. That gathering of like-minded souls feels refreshing compared to the rest of our week's work necessities. And the lesson of the day can prove valuable to our lives for days to come. It is all so familiar, so recognizable, that though we may have brief gratitude for the purpose of the assembly, it is too rote to have much in the way of lasting significance.

Yet when we are exploring new ideas: comprehending new languages, learning music, and new instruments, there is a magic that happens. We find ourselves inspired. Suddenly we are not having to memorize or remember new conjugations. It is not about figuring out what note comes next. Unexpectedly there arises an understanding causing that language or music or instruments to become a part of us. We find inspiration in what we have already accomplished and cannot wait to learn and absorb more and more. Our new venture is captivating to our minds and souls, and we discover a new source of joy, of love, and appreciation. We experience gratitude for that knowledge to have come into our lives.

If it is a new language, seeking out ways to use our newfound skill comes naturally. Perhaps there is a club, others with whom we can have dialogue, or places for us to travel. If we find there is music in us, it will come out as we find ourselves tapping our fingers or feet whenever there is music around. We will not even realize we are doing it much of the time, but when we look around, we realize not everyone taps out the beat. Perhaps we will write our own tunes? We have a special fondness or love that others do not have. We have a gift for appreciating music, harmony, and composition.

If something is true, it is always true. That is what universal truth is. Consequently, the above learning scenarios work the same way relationships work, and the same way knowing God works. Should we want to know more about any person or any subject, we need to spend time researching, learning, and practicing. Once a week just does not cut it.

Finding the inspiration to know more about one's religion or one's spirituality requires commitment too. To be a good person requires practice. To be a good anything entails preparation and rehearsal. The desire to habitually engage with the Father must be cultivated. This requires that we bring our desire into our consciousness. Just like the inspiration we get from learning new languages, sports, or musical instruments. We work at it willingly and joyously. We practice and learn from it daily. We find others who share in it, and in the end, we find ourselves blessed by it.

65

Broken Record

ಸಿ ಲ

Soul Gardening focuses on our relationship with the Master Gardener. Our Creator. Our Father. For what is better than for us to celebrate where we all came from, and whose laws we abide by?

The Lord created for us an endless universe. Yes, an incomprehensibly limitless cosmos that by all scientific standards is continuing to expand. Have you ever considered the size of the universe?

Just our little solar system which consists of the sun, and its orbiting planets, along with all the numerous moons, asteroids, comets, etc., is well beyond our imagination in size and scope. Talk about infinity. Our sun is more than 100 times larger than our Earth and is just one star amongst the hundreds of billions of stars in the Milky Way galaxy. Our universe so far, has more than three hundred billion large galaxies just like the Milky Way. Our world, this space we live in, contains billions and trillion of stars. I did say incomprehensibly limitless, didn't I?

And yet as we explore the infinitesimal microscopic universe in the other direction, we find we have to keep building greater and more powerful magnification tools to see the universe built into the most minute particle.

Science once told us that the atom was the smallest particle in the universe. But it was later discovered that quarks are smaller still. Quarks combine with each other to create protons and neutrons which are the parts of an atom we learned about long ago. Spend a few minutes thinking about this wide range of sizes and worlds and consider the incredible consciousness that could conceive of and then create an entire universe such as ours.

Science is wonderful. It has explained all the above information to us. Science, remember, is the methodical study of all the structures and all the behaviors of our physical and natural world. But what we forget sometimes is that science is a process of observation. In other words, science is only able to observe what God has already created. Think about that! This magical and spectacularly beautiful universe is here for our discovery as well as for our pleasure and delight.

God. The ultimate Master Gardener. The One we get to have a relationship with. Some still wonder how to have this type of close relationship. You are encouraged to find what resonates with you. Read. Listen. We need to open our hearts and minds to what is already here for us to discover. Once we find the astonishing beauty of God's creations, it is hard to imagine we would not want to get in touch.

66

Feeding Your Soul

೫◌౷

As we enter this Thanksgiving week, I have a prayer for us all...

Dearest Lord,

With Thy guidance it is my prayer that we, each seeking You in our own way, have spent much time feeding our souls by planting and cultivating love. That the expression of such has given us an inward view of ourselves with abundant understanding and forgiveness.

May we have given time to finding peace within ourselves and may we have found joy in life itself.

May we have nurtured truth and compassion in ourselves and others. May we have found wisdom to the point where we understand that our beliefs lead us to how we will treat all others: those that agree with us, and those that do not.

May we now have the understanding that our own fears and anger actually hurt our bodies and our minds, and may we have worked to enrich our lives by practicing kindness. May we have learned to live in the moment as much as possible.

May we have weeded from our lives what others want and expect from us and developed a true knowing of who our authentic selves really are. May we love and approve of ourselves, as we also remember that each one of us is a part of humanity.

In this fresh harvest, may we share all good things with those who are in any need. May we show others a positive attitude with which to face the world.

And with Thy blessing, may we always remember to be ever thankful and grateful for everything in our lives.

Amen.

HAPPY THANKSGIVING!

67

It's the Holiday Season

୨୦ଓଃ

When Black Friday and Cyber Monday are more popular than Christmas Eve services...You know this is true. By the time Christmas arrives, we have worn ourselves out shopping for bigger and better things we probably do not need. We have partied until the cows came home. And then finally decided we are too pooped to celebrate the reason for the season.

Christmas songs send light and love into the dark crevices of our personalities and open the window to vulnerability. To that place where our greatest compassion lives almost in fear of being discovered. For along with that compassion is our truly open heart. And that is where love lives.

Love makes us vulnerable. It opens us to feeling old wounds, and the fear of getting hurt with new ones. Being vulnerable can be frightening because it makes us feel defenseless, helpless, and weak. We feel exposed, and at risk.

How can this be true if love is supposed to be the answer to life? The answer to everything?

Well, love is the answer, yet like most things in this life, love takes practice and persistence too. And let us not forget that love goes and comes in many directions.

Were it only the case that we truly learned about receiving and being loved as infants and children. Yet, even with that foundation, we would have to be practicing and learning still as adults.

First, the true love of self resolves an awful lot of things. Love of self should be accompanied by self-understanding, which of course, gives way to self-compassion and self-forgiveness. If we could master these things, we would be laying a great foundation for our own lives, as well developing our ability to love others. Enough of this self-love and our hearts would learn to not be injured too easily.

Then we need practice in loving others, and how to rebound when others hurt us. Receiving love is yet another chapter in the narrative of our lives.

But it is the Holiday Season, and often we reach out to show love to others way before we have learned to love ourselves. We want to love but cannot seem to give our love freely enough. No, we all seem to want to get something back. Don't think so? How many times have you mentioned to someone else the good deed you did for another? When is the last time you dropped big cash without that tax write off receipt? Who have you said a silent prayer for lately? See, there are all kinds of ways to show love.

Maybe we are just imitating what we have learned along the way which is to expect something in return? Maybe we expect respect or understanding? Perhaps we require acknowledgement for the gift? Do we anticipate that our love will be returned? It is hard to give love and truly envisage nothing back.

Love is the answer. And it starts with us. Try loving yourself the way God loves you: with all your freckles, bowed knees, and thin lips. God loves us with all our mistakes, and faults, and misgivings. He loves us with our lack of compassion and our bad moods. He loves us when we talk to Him and even when we don't. God loves us for who we are. Our authentic selves, and the person we show the world as well.

Want a great gift for Christmas? Give yourself the gift of loving yourself. Imagine the possibilities that love provides when you are the giver and the receiver. It just might be one of the greatest gifts you get (and give) this Christmas season!

68

Anticipation

❦

Holidays...it is the hurry up and wait season...

Getting out early and standing in the cold waiting for the stores to open...
Driving to the airport three hours early and waiting for the plane...
Sitting in the car and waiting for the traffic to clear...
Smelling the turkey/ham/roast and waiting for it to be done...
Planning the party for weeks, and waiting for the guests to arrive...
And then, just waiting for the good time to start.

Expecting only goodness and joy because it is that time of year...

The time to listen to joyous music, and then sing along...
Time to throw some change into that Salvation Army bucket...

> Time to hold the door open for the next person...
> Time to smile as we run errands, and say Merry Christmas!

Hopes are high for all the gatherings of friends and family. Everything will be just fine this year if only because...

> There is a new baby in the family...
> There is a new puppy to fawn over...
> Everyone is well this year...
> So and So is coming in after many months or years away...
> So and So is ill and everyone will be on their best behavior...

Cut to reality. We all suffer from having expectations. That favorable prospect of good things and wonderful times. The joyful anticipatory feeling filled with hope. And as the time fast approaches for the event we are looking forward to, the expectations grow, but so does that little sense of dread. Which we quickly push to the back of our minds, and with bated breath go back to the confidence and likelihood of positivity.

Time, dear friends, to take a deep breath and let all those expectations go. Letting go of every hope and every fear that we put on people and things. Yes, let them go. The crazy, selfish, wonderful, loud, quiet, annoying, cackling, nosey people that you could not wait to see. Let them be exactly who they are. For they too have expectations. And trust me, our unmet expectations can ruin anything.

So, let us bring in the reason for the season. Bring on the compassion, the forgiveness, and the love. And remember the whole point of gathering.

We congregate to mark the passing of time...
To celebrate this glorious season...
To have the best meal of the year...
To remember those loved ones we have lost...
To celebrate all the new additions to the group...
And let us not forget that very special One whose birth we celebrate!

Let us take our cues from Joy to the World:[21]

"Joy to the world, the Lord has come!
Let Earth receive her King
Let every heart prepare Him room
And Heaven and nature sing
And Heaven and nature sing
And Heaven, and Heaven, and nature sing

Joy to the World, the Savior reigns!
Let men their songs employ
While fields and floods, rocks, hills and plains
Repeat the sounding joy
Repeat the sounding joy
Repeat, repeat, the sounding joy

No more let sins and sorrows grow
Nor thorns infest the ground
He comes to make His blessings flow
Far as the curse is found
Far as the curse is found
Far as, far as, the curse is found

He rules the world with truth and grace
And makes the nations prove
The glories of His righteousness
And wonders of His love

And wonders of His love
And wonders, wonders, of His love"

Isn't this what we are really anticipating? And won't all our expectations be met? Yes indeed!

69

Where are you Christmas?

ഇരു

There actually are sad Christmas songs. We all have our struggles, and Christmas seems to bring them to the forefront because we are supposed to be happy this time of year. We have difficulty handling the stress of our day-to-day lives, even though those tasks are simply a part of our civilized world. We are bone-tired because we devote too much time to working, but if we do not do that, we will not be keeping our jobs. We find it hard to make ends meet, as money doesn't go as far as it used to, and let's face it, it is not like costs are coming down. Doctor bills and medicines are a burden, even with insurance. And the chunk of change that comes out of a paycheck first? The taxes and then rent or mortgage payments that keep a roof over our heads.

That list is not even counting the times when there is trouble at work or at home. Adulting is not easy. Grownups can act out like five-year olds, and some bosses have no idea how to manage. Hard physical labor wears down the human body. Then there are the bullies at the kid's school, and the friends and family who are demanding and critical, and never helpful or supportive. Just getting along can weigh us down.

Civilization comes stocked with many burdens, and we feel incredible anguish a lot. We feel our lives should be easier, and we virtually demand compassion from our loved ones because we often feel we are suffering. Expectations are frequently hard to fulfill, and we find ourselves filled with melancholy.

But then someone we know becomes ill. Maybe it is a life-threatening disease, or a recurrence of such. It could be any manner of addiction that strikes seemingly out of the blue. Perhaps the law was broken, and we have to get involved with the judiciary. These are, or quickly become painfully personal and emotional. These are the struggles that neither time nor money can fix. These personal afflictions are the most wearing to us, because they touch our lives and the lives of those we dearly love. And often we are lost trying to find our way through. It feels that we are adrift and wondering, rather than focused and secure.

There are struggles we are afraid to converse about. Struggles we are terrified to imagine even on our worst day. Situations we find ourselves in that are contrary to the way we want our lives or our world to be. They are, for example, our struggle against our fear of death and dying, against terror attacks, and the wildfires and floods we hear about all too often.

How do we find enough compassion for these, when the larger world, that is very much a part of our lives too, is dealing with a terrifying amount of anger and hate? Riots and wars are not calming down. Children need so much more than we give them. Populations are shifting as people run away from violence to uncertain futures and questionable welcoming committees. Can you remember a world with so much bigotry?

The struggles are frightening and overwhelming. And you and I are just trying to get by every day while having a soft pillow, a comfortable bed, and having a roof over our heads. We wonder if all this can ever get fixed. How do we unearth adequate empathy in today's world for the millions of people suffering on such a massive scale?

This is not meant to bring us down. It is a reality we face. Because it is Christmas, we must first remember all of our many blessings. The love and gratefulness of remembering them will carry our compassion and forgiveness forward. We must remember there is hope in the air this season. There is promise, and there is charity. We need to simply do what we are able to do and give what we are able to give.

Providing some assistance to others, often puts our own difficulties into perspective. Paraphrasing Proverbs 14:31... To help the poor is to honor God. So, let us offer what we can to others. Let us look at our world with compassion. Let kind-heartedness be our guide. Send a card; make a phone call. Recognize that prayer changes things. Empathize. Become benevolent in thoughts and deeds. Keep the Lord your God in your heart. For that is where Christmas has always lived. It lives in our love-filled hearts.

70

What's Missing?

༄༅

Teachers are being beaten up in their classrooms...
More than 2 million people are in jail in the United States. That is more than any other country in the world...
Opioid and alcohol addiction is rampant...
Homelessness is ubiquitous...
Social media and smart device overuse is widespread...
Religious conflicts and extremism are in the news daily...
Food and water contamination is prevalent...
There is a lack of education in our civilized world...
We witness safety and security issues way too often...
Conflicts and wars are still going on...
There are accountability issues everywhere...
And millions of people are running away from violence and horrors we cannot even imagine...
In many countries, laws are made taking away freedoms because of fear...

You certainly do not have to agree with me on that list, but something is missing. We see and feel the greed. Everything, especially at Christmas is me, me, me. Bigger, better, stronger, faster. We are pressured to follow suit. We want to. We are told we need 'things' to make us happy, and we believe the advertisements. Our neighbors sure seem happy with all their stuff.

Have we really forgotten the values that truly matter? Probably not, but we might just see them on a much smaller scale. We care about our family and friends. We love them. Are they safe? Are they well? Are they happy? Okay, now we can focus elsewhere.

Where in that picture does loving God and loving others fit? We are taught that love, joy, peace, kindness, goodness, faithfulness, and gentleness are the fruits of the Holy Spirit, and that our love must be sincere. I surely prefer lots of love and peace and kindness, more than I want a bigger television.

What is missing is our having a sense of caring for humanity and having compassion for each other. The issues are so large, we are overwhelmed. We are told that one person matters and makes a difference, but that is someone other than who we feel we are. There is just too much going on right here and right now in our lives to even think about changing the world.

Yet there is Good News. Jesus is coming! Not only in the sense of His second coming, but in the sense of our celebration of His birth. A reminder every year that we are not to be daunted by the enormity of the world's grief.

We can do this now: We can be kind, and we can be gracious. We can start the work of compassion and generosity. We are not responsible to complete the work, but neither are we allowed to ignore or abandon it.

Yes, Jesus is coming. Let our hearts be filled with love and light. And let us share it with the world.

71

"Tis the Season

☙❧

Two billion Christians celebrate the birth of Jesus on December 25th each year. We do this though we are unsure exactly when He was born. We do not even know the year for certain.

Speculation is that His birth was more likely in the spring or the fall of the year, or perhaps that it is related to the Jewish celebration of the Feast of Tabernacles. The winter solstice may even play a part in setting the date. Still others add nine months to March 25th, which is supposed to be the day of the Annunciation. That is when Mary was told of her part in this greatest story ever told.

Early Christians are said to have celebrated Christmas on January 6th. More than likely due to the old Julien calendar shifting eleven days after the world moved to the Gregorian calendar. Most European churches continue to combine Epiphany and nativity celebrations on January 6th. In some parts of the United Kingdom, January 6th is referred to as "Old Christmas."

Constantine, the first Roman Emperor converted to Christianity, is said to have celebrated Christmas on December 25th. It was he who commissioned the Church of the Nativity to be built in Bethlehem in the same location where Jesus was born. Some years later, Pope Julius I officially declared Christ's birth to be December 25th.[22]

So here we are...officially December 25th. But what's in a day? It is the marking of time, and the opportunity to create memories. It is tradition. It is a time when friends and families gather for a shared meal. It is when hash marks are put on a wall to see how tall the kids have gotten. A time to try to remember how grandma used to make stuffing, and how grandad carved the bird. A time for all to file into church wearing our Sunday best, and sing of the joy of this night and this day.

It is the dimming of the church lights while candles alone light the sanctuary, as we all sing Silent Night through tears of the purest joy. Because Jesus has come... in His innocence and in His glory. He is the Light of the world after all.

Haven't we found that there are daily reasons to celebrate the birth of our Lord? Isn't that, in essence what we do each day when we converse with Him in prayer... celebrating the birth of His Son? Of course, it is.

For this moment, in this day, let us forget the tinsel and the mistletoe. Let us celebrate, the meaning of which is to raise, let us celebrate and rejoice with the greatest pleasure, the greatest love the world knows. Let us do it with this beautiful carol: "O Holy Night."[23]

Oh Holy Night
The stars are brightly shining
It is the night of our dear saviour's birth
Long lay the world
In sin and error pining
Til he appeared and the soul felt it's worth
A thrill of hope
The weary world rejoices
For yonder breaks a new and glorious morn
Fall on your knees

Oh hear the angel voices
Oh night divine
Oh night, when Christ was born
Oh night divine
Oh night, oh night divine

72

I Surrender All

෨෮

There is one thing I do on every January first. I give my coming year to the Lord and ask that He use me as an instrument to do His work. I rarely have told even my closet friends about this, as I used to keep private feelings very close to the vest. (Remember that I lied to my minister over a prayer...) Writing this book has changed all that, as I have come to feel much more open about most things.

This tradition of mine has been going on yearly for some twenty years, and I must admit, it took a very, very long time to be able to do it with a sincere and fully committed heart. This is not something I do lightly, or even really meant for the first several years. It frightened me. It is something, however, that I wanted to be able to do.

You have heard of faking it until you make it? That is exactly what I did. I went through the motions and said my speech. And when another year went by and the world hadn't crashed around me, I said, "Whew!" and did it again.

I have learned to be more committed now and can fling my arms open into surrender as I offer Him my next year. It is a process: and I have learned my whole life is just that. Definitely something for all of us to think about...

Here is a song I love:

> All to Jesus I surrender,
> All to Him I freely give;
> I will ever love and trust Him,
> In His presence daily live.
>
> Refrain:
> I surrender all,
> I surrender all;
> All to Thee, my blessed Savior,
> I surrender all.
>
> All to Jesus I surrender,
> Humbly at His feet I bow;
> Worldly pleasures all forsaken,
> Take me, Jesus, take me now.
>
> All to Jesus I surrender,
> Make me, Savior, wholly Thine;
> Let me feel the Holy Spirit,
> Truly know that Thou art mine.
>
> All to Jesus I surrender,
> Lord, I give myself to Thee;
> Fill me with Thy love and power,
> Let Thy blessing fall on me.
>
> All to Jesus I surrender.
> Now I feel the sacred flame;
> Oh, the joy of full salvation!
> Glory, glory, to His Name![24]

73

WYSIWYG

☙❧

For those of you who may have forgotten (or never heard the term), WYSIWYG means What You See Is What You Get. In the early days of computers this referred to getting in a print-out exactly what one saw on the computer screen. This acronym, I believe, applies to life.

Remember the story about the man who climbed up to his roof to escape a merciless flood? He kept waiting and waiting for God to save him. The man had several opportunities to be rescued. First a log floated by, but the fellow let it go. He told himself "God is going to save me!" Then a small boat with just a couple people in it came by, and they encouraged the man to get in. He refused, again saying God was going to save him. Time went by and the waters rose. A news helicopter spotted the man on the roof and dropped a rescue line. But once again the man refused, waiving off the helicopter, steadfastly believing his God would save him. Unfortunately, the deluge continued, the waters climbed, and the man drowned. Meeting the Lord in heaven, the man asked God why He didn't save him in the flood. And God said, "I sent a log, a boat, and a helicopter!"

What do we expect from God? Because we believe, should we expect our lives to be filled with joy and happiness and riches? Do we expect not to suffer, to not have loss or despair? And we probably expect to witness miracles often too. Let us really think about this. What do we expect from knowing God and welcoming Him into our lives?

I obviously have a God thing going on in this life. This is not something I can explain necessarily. It a choice I have made. But this choice has helped me more than any other choice I have ever made. He is where I look to first, whether it is for strength I need or if I have a problem to solve. I just say, please help me, or please guide me, Lord, to find the support or solution I need here. And then I do my very best to let go and try to remain fluid with what is happening around me.

Now that doesn't mean I sit and wait for a telegram from heaven.

Sometimes I do get a flash of a scathingly brilliant idea: something I had not thought of before. Of course, I assume there is Divine Intervention happening. Often it is a lot less direct. And sometimes, I am just lost in searching for a solution. But I keep thinking and planning and trying to come up with what might be the best thing for me to do to handle the situation. In other words, I do actually pursue a solution. Blockages come and I shift direction, always asking for guidance. I believe that the smoother plans happen, the better choice it is.

Here is a recent example. Just last year I was forced to move from a place and city I loved. My rent quintupled. Yes, this is a painfully true story! In a month I had to find what to do and where to go with all my earthly possessions. Years and years of stuff, as well as treasures from generations of my family, all tucked away in every nook and cranny of my place.

It felt like every single idea I had, whether it was donating furniture, to hire or not hire a mover, how to possibly get the move accomplished in the shortest amount of time, was filled with roadblocks. The companies I wanted to deal with would not call me back or did not want my donation. Some wanted the donation but would not come to my zip code to pick it up. Others were willing, but it would take those two plus months to get to me.

Movers I did not want to deal with were happy to give me quotes without even knowing what I needed to move, and the moving companies I thought would be better choices would not make an appointment for a quote except during the work week when I was working in another city. It all felt messy and defeating and impossible.

When the notice first came out, the first thing I did, (once I caught my breath) was thank God for the opportunity. Then I asked for His blessing, and to guide me through it, keeping me safe along the way. Because of this, despite all the roadblocks and obstructions along the way, I did not panic. When the naysayers got in my way, I just took a different tack, believing all the way that I was guided... because I had asked to be guided, and therefore, I trusted that I was.

The move went more smoothly than I could ever have imagined and in a shorter period of time than I can now believe happened. Things started falling into place miraculously. People seemed to come out of the woodwork to assist with tasks, and aid in the process. And in the end, a hundred times or more, I said THANK YOU, GOD!!!

You would be amazed at the wondrous outcomes I have witnessed, that in retrospect were set into motion years in advance of them happening. When the time is right – magic happens. Do you see or feel this happening in your own life? Are you asking for help or guidance from Him?

You may say that I see things with a tainted perspective, and you would be correct in that assessment. So, I would have to ask you...how do you view this life? As a crap shoot or a roll of the dice? Think you could view this as an opportunity to be a spiritual tourist on planet Earth? What would it take for you to feel yourself as a beloved child of God?

WYSIWYG...Check out quantum physics some time. You just wait until you get to the part where the researchers were expecting to see specific phenomenon in a light box experiment. They scientifically decide what they believe they should see the lights doing. And when they looked, the lights behaved just that way. Then when the experimenters change their expectation, that new expectancy is precisely what they then saw. And it happened over and over. They saw exactly what they wanted to see from the light patterns each time.

Yes, I have a God thing. I choose to follow Him. I further invite Him into my heart, into my mind, and try to live my life from that standpoint. Notice please: I say try. I am still my human self after all and do my best to set my intentions and aim for the goal. I have just learned the journey can be very different than what I had in mind.

God is where my guidance comes from. I ask for it. I place my life firmly in His hands to do with as He pleases. I make a point of it every year to tell Him this coming year is His.

I surrender all, and I choose to have Him whisper to me every single day...especially when I need help or some guidance. I seek His counsel, and I do my best to look for Him in every person, and every situation I am in.

I am not perfect, and He knows that. I can be a real jerk sometimes, but I am doing the best I can, and have seen so many blessings in my life because of this perspective. What I see is a world blessed by a God who, though omnipotent, waits for us to see and know Him. And when we do, we will see Him in everything!

74

So Many Paths

☙❧

But where are they leading? Not everyone agrees that there are many paths to God. We are all seeking something and are on the path to somewhere. But do all paths lead to God eventually?

Beyond one's desires for a loving relationship, a safe place to live, and enough money, what else do we seek for our lives? It feels we have inadvertently created a world where instant gratification is what we think we need in our lives. People are bored if not quenched straightaway. We seek adventure, entertainment, and diversion from tedium, because we are world-weary of any type of constraint. Spontaneous and unrestricted uninhibitedness promise us 21st century happiness.

In this same hurry up environment, we often rush to judgment. We are used to making split-second decisions. We have opinions which we do not hesitate to share on social media. Life has become a harsh contest for who has more vacations, events, and celebrations they must attend. Yet if a moment of silence inadvertently appears, we reach for a device to connect us to the Internet to check in.

It is like we cannot be alone with ourselves. It was not that long ago if we just needed a break from all the hubbub, we could just pretend we forgot about something on our 'to do' list. We cannot get away with that now what with smartphones and other devices that remind us every second.

Consequently, we no longer seek silence and peace. Oh, we crave a twenty-minute nap now and again, or a quick break from an intense workout. But more than that we can hardly tolerate.

Beyond these desires we have, that may take some time to attain and maintain, our civilization has pushed us into fast, speedy, hurry hurry, rush rush, with something always expected of us to do, or be, and it is rarely what we want to do or be. But it is not easy to set one's own path and then follow it. Not when acceptance is one of a human's primal needs. Social acceptance and rejection are at the core of our being. Many of us are on paths to nowhere because we have no idea what truly makes us tick and makes us happy. We follow others path's because we are accepted and liked and are included in the merrymaking.

Where is your path taking you? Perhaps it is time to start seeking our own path? To find our true course, we need to find out who we truly are authentically. This is something that does not just happen instantaneously because we have figured out that is our desire. It takes time and dedication. The same goes for spirituality or Christianity or Judaism or any of the other thousands of faiths out there. There is wisdom that can be learned from them all, but only if we jump on that path for a spell.

Because we want the benefits of these practices, we cannot just wish them into our lives. They take practice. They take time and dedication. They take learning and experiencing. We cannot just read a book and bingo everything changes. We must take it all in emotionally, to begin the healing journey.

Let us stop being too busy and too self-absorbed. For we shall reap in our lives exactly what we sow. Let us seek what is missing from our lives with the same dedication we have for our other interests. Let us quench our internal thirst for meaning in our lives, rather than continue to suffer from spiritual dehydration. Please Lord, let us find our true selves and our desire to seek Thee with all of our hearts. Follow God's path and allow Him to guide your life.

75

The Devil is in the Detail

☙❧

In case you are wondering that idiom means that there is something mysterious hidden in the details. Something that may seem very simple, might well be more convoluted than initially expected.

Perhaps because there was a good deal of drama in my childhood, I have always tried to negotiate and make peace with unpleasant disparities in my life. Entering the business world, it was a talent to be able to negotiate differences whether between people or companies, finding similarities where others struggled to find them. My fascination with religion began as a teenager, but fast-forward to adulthood, and the attraction became ever stronger. What is it we all want in life, if we seek a deeper meaning through religion? Certainly, there must be something universal about all these religions that draws us into following them?

That is what I looked forward to deciphering, by exploring different religious practices. Not surprisingly, I was not the first to seek and to find that most religions, and spirituality for that matter, attempt to show man how to search for god. They also teach us how to please the gods and or goddesses at the root of the belief by sacrificing and performing good deeds. Man must reach out to find and please these gods. It is always up to man to satisfy and gratify these deities.

Believing in heaven and hell are principles that have faded from popularity. Now people seek something more modern. We do not want commandments and rules. We now want spiritual teachers to explain and clarify that which we want to hear. We want them to justify our own passions for how we would like religion to be. We decide what the truth is that will validate our spiritual desires. We look to be entertained by those who claim to have the answers.

We start to believe that all the gods and goddesses of all the religions are equal and the same. Some of us even hope they are, because we long for the fighting and the arguing and the animosity between faiths to stop. We want the hate to stop.

All religions are not the same. What they do have are dissimilar tenets that contradict one another, and unique gods and goddesses who are appeased in distinctive ways. The gods people serve and try to please are not the same; they are not even similar. Proclaiming that all gods from all religions are alike is inaccurate.

Consider Christianity. Let us look at this two-thousand-year-old religion that separates itself from all the rest. Christianity has a God, a Supreme Being, who is eternal, and has created everything in our world. This God has a divine nature, and a love of humanity so intense that He gives us free will to decide on our own, how we choose to live. This God is love. He reaches out for us, not the other way around. In fact, we cannot impress the Christian God by being well-meaning people, or by our labors, or by performing good deeds. Even if we do them in His name. The Christian God has so much love for us that He waits for us to reach out to find Him.

He has provided His son to us so that we might understand His love. Jesus, the Son of God, makes all the difference. And if we get to know and accept Jesus Christ, we will have a better understanding of love. The Christian God gifts us with mercy and the grace of forgiveness for our sins through Jesus.

You see, all the other religions teach man that his job is to search for god and try to gain his favor. With Christianity, God is here with us. He is waiting and watching for us to make the first move. Waiting for us to accept His love, His forgiveness, His grace, and His mercy. His love is everlasting and will provide us with peace within ourselves that will envelop our lives. The words are not always easy to take in and believe. They are powerful and so full of promise that often they seem too good to be true. Yet once the truth becomes a part of our hearts, there is no denying the power of the greatest love the world has ever known.

Religions are not the same. But each man and woman make the choice on their amazing singular journey to seek and follow God if they so choose.

If you are searching, would you rather have to work to please a god? Or would you consider looking for the God who is waiting for you to discover Him, so He can put blessings into your life?

Perhaps it is God who is in the details?

76

Potholes on the Road to Enlightenment

☙❧

Once we embrace the love of the Lord and decide to live with a fully loving heart, there is no turning back. Our lives change from that moment on and will never be the same again. We veer toward the road to our own enlightenment. The highway looks promising. We have the Lord in our heart, and a goal of peace and awareness in mind. So, we venture forth with as much positivity as we can muster.

We explore why people are the way they are, and why we ourselves are the way we are. This encourages the gradual discovery of our authentic selves. Our mind connects to our soul, and we decide to follow the road less traveled. Our souls hear the call, and a spark of the divine within is felt; perhaps for the first time. We launch ourselves toward the on ramp. We embrace God in a new and exciting way. The very thought of peace, being loved, and living our values is highly seductive, so we put the pedal to the metal and rush headlong onto the wholeness highway.

What once was the frustration of the same lesson repeated over and over and over again, now becomes the blessing of the same lesson repeated, until we finally learn from it, and that lesson becomes a part of who we are. We change, and do not need to have that lesson repeated.

We find blessings everywhere and learn to be grateful for the small miracles we see each and every day. Even if the miracle is a reminder of a painful childhood or experience along life's path, because we have learned that the only way to discover the joy of our true selves is sometimes through the pain we once felt. We appreciate that our human bodies are filled with emotions we once thought embarrassing; others that are loud, some that are wet, and still more that can feel fierce when compared to the habits we once had of holding them inside. But we become thankful that they exist as it reminds us that we are experiencing the fullness of life.

We comprehend that the senses of seeing, hearing, smelling, touching, and tasting are simply the first five we learned. We come to rely on intuition and insight, and we have the blessed experience that those two never fail us as they are gifts from God.

Suddenly we uncover questions we never thought of before: What would Jesus do? What did God intend? What do I really believe? Can I accept that I am beloved? We find we have additional goals in life to understand, and to find meaning and purpose. We appreciate intention and awareness. We wish we could explain that concept to our friends. To those not on the same path, intention is meaningless, unless it has to do with money, fame or power. We may lose some of those we love because they just cannot open up to our new way of being, nor can they comprehend our newly discovered inner happiness and peace. Sometimes we feel the loneliness of this singular journey.

We discover what we believe and what we do not and wonder why there is so much contradiction in the two. We also learn that there are many different kinds of healing, and that healing can hurt. We discover there is a big difference between pain and suffering.

Gratitude overcomes us occasionally, and we find compassion and empathy are easier to offer than they used to be. We become more mindful. The highway slows down sometimes with construction zones so we may process what we are going through on the journey.

Roadblocks show up as anxiety, depression, unworthiness, guilt, and sometimes resentment. And there are issues to deal with that may stop our progress for a while. Detours of fear and sorrow occur.

We find prayer and meditation are like rest stops, and we find inner peace and harmony to be as precious as we ever dreamed they would be.

But there are shortcuts on the road too as we detect our inner voices of love, compassion, forgiveness, and acceptance. This thoroughfare we are on is completely a no passing zone; because we eventually realize everything is happening at exactly the right moment in time, and we need not be attached to the outcome of any situation. Every path and detour has a purpose for our higher good.

Yes, whoever said there is no turning back once you plant your feet on the path to enlightenment was absolutely right. Along the way we may struggle, and we may weep, but finally learn that we are worth all the breakdowns. We gain the knowledge and understanding that we are treasured. And then we weep some more.

The search for meaning and purpose can be long and hard, but it will come to us. There are many roadblocks and traffic jams. This road to increased spirituality is filled with cracks, rocks, construction, potholes, and what seems like too many detours. The road has no tolls, yet we will pay a high price. But the journey will result in our discovery that we are beloved.

77

How Deep is Your Love?

෩ ෪

Valentine's Day is fast approaching. A day when flowers, cards and cherubs will fill our minds, it feels appropriate to speak of love. Those Valentine's and flowers are symbols of love and caring; of devotion and affection we have for one another. People with significant others will fill restaurants on that day, as singles will lament that they are all alone. In all reality, and if we are fortunate, we will each find our way to some chocolate.

But my question about how deep our love may be is not related to the Feast of St. Valentine. It is related to one's love of God. How deep is that love? Is it measurable? Does our love go beyond the doctrine we were taught? Does our love of the Lord go beyond what any church or religious leader tells us it should be? Or does it begin and end there? I am wondering if we ever thought about that.

We have ventured into this area in past stories: that even within the same sects of religions, interpretations can vary. Between preachers, explanations differ. Even when religious texts are involved in controversies, the various translations disagree. When the basis of a religion is the Holy Bible with

Old and New Testaments, the number of books within each Testament is different. So, where does that leave us? Should we just avoid these contradictions? Do we hold fast and decide whatever faith we follow is the right one?

Religious writings are just a part of faith: guidelines if you will. When asked how deep your love of God is, the real question may be how profound is that love? Is it bottomless? Is it a secret? Is it robust and resilient? What can it withstand?

Can it endure a direct question from a friend or foe? Are we able to bear witness? These questions are not asked to judge, rather for introspective purposes.

How about controversy. There are judgments made about faith based upon argument, atheism, historical facts, newly discovered documents, zealots, and more. What are our choices? Do we stick to what we learned and understood as a child? Do we learn Hebrew and to speak Aramaic to try to research on our own? Do we ignore anything other than what our beliefs allow for us to feel safe with? Perhaps we just get angry at the challenge.

Or, can we develop our love of the Lord into a faith so robust and durable that it transcends anything that may come along? If we can intensify our passion to the point where we are steadfast and our faith is resolute, then nothing can make us waiver. And it is not because we refuse to entertain the new information. It is because we can say to ourselves, what if this new information were true? How does that affect my love, my devotion, my tenderness for my Father in Heaven?

Does our love change if Judas was not the villain he was portrayed to be? Does it change us or our beliefs if it turns out that Jesus had a wife? Does that alter our convictions in any way?

What would need to be adjusted in the world we know, or how we live our lives, if it were proven that Eve did not disobey God by eating the fruit of the tree of knowledge of good and evil? What if it was not an apple?

What if God loves every single person equally and unconditionally? How would that transform our perspective of things?

Is our faith really breakable by a few stories being different than what we thought they were? Or can our faith and our love of God be revised to be larger, with much greater potency?

Consider the power of love...

78

Finding Your Sweet Spot

❧☙

"Who loves ya, baby?" That was the catchphrase that came to life in the character of Kojak,[25] a TV cop played by Telly Savalas from the mid-1970's. Kojak was a tough guy with a big heart, who beat up on bad guys while sucking on a lollipop.

So, the question of the day is, who loves you? Loves you and you know it and you feel it. And who do you love that deeply, that completely?

That love in our lives, the kind we really feel with every part of our being, brings us a calmness. It brings a peace, and a softening of our whole body. Melting us if you will, into the pure joy of the love that has been offered to us. A love that relaxes any tension out of our entire being and allows us to exhale from whatever pressures we have been feeling.

Add to that devotion, that there are no demands, limits, expectations or boundaries, and we find unconditional love. The rarest of all love is to have and feel this sensation where, regardless of circumstance, the love that expects nothing in return, is there for us. As human beings we long for this kind of feeling. We may even have it from time to time when we first fall in love with another. But this kind of affection is not always easy to conceptualize, let alone experience fully for any time period.

This is unselfish love, where one cares more for the other's feeling of happiness than for oneself; where it is not subject to any terms or conditions. This is bliss. The closest we can come is a mother's love for her children. It is a mother's instinct that all of her emotional feelings and all of her devotion be bestowed upon her offspring.

If we would like to find that sweet spot of a blessed existence, it is most important for us to love ourselves unconditionally. The world around us is often critical and sometimes dangerous. Society enjoys assessing the worth of its peoples and putting those verdicts on display. The tough skin needed to survive what we call civilization, must withstand a lot these days. But underneath, we need to develop the wisdom and acumen of our own self-worth and value.

It is essential that we cultivate an acceptance of all our human faults and weaknesses. Regardless of circumstance, our own support and unconditional love of ourselves is paramount to being able to love another.

Gratitude can be a great starting point. Being thankful for and appreciating the beauty of our natural surroundings. The flora and the fauna of the countryside for example. Recognizing the vastness of the universe, and all that it entails. Trying to comprehend the staggering exquisiteness of all life forms. These thoughts can illuminate to us just how tiny we are in the world, yet it may also remind us that our difficulties in life may not be large or devastating after all.

Perspective is really everything. Can we imagine loving ourselves unconditionally? Can we conceive that we can be loved absolutely? Can we allow ourselves to be worthy of that?

Love is amazing in its power. Love can heal many ills. It can cure loneliness, despair, and fear. Love can cure hopelessness. And we have to let it in, in order to allow it to work its magic.

If we can acknowledge and accept our perceived imperfections and failings, by comprehending that all humans have flaws, we can get past the blame and unworthiness so many of us feel for ourselves. Learning to do this will heal us and therefore help us get to the place where we can accept love being given to us.

Humans try to love unconditionally. We have feelings and emotions and regrets and jealousy that can get in the way. But God can and does love us unconditionally and completely. We humans long to experience that kind of approval and acknowledgement. We do not always know how to take it all in, because we do not think it is possible.

Knowing that God loves you can be overwhelming. It will be the sweet spot in your life to know that and experience it completely with your body and your soul. The expression of that love will bring tears to your eyes and cause your heart to leap with everlasting joy. You will never be the same again, because you will now be able to go through life knowing you are worthy of His love, just as you are.

Look up and listen to this song I grew up with, that to this day brings me joy through tears of knowing that I am accepted and loved by Him. Take the words and their meaning into your heart. The song is "Just as I Am."[26]

> Just as I am, without one plea,
> But that Thy blood was shed for me,
> And that Thou bid'st me come to Thee,
> O Lamb of God, I come! I come!
>
> Just as I am, and waiting not
> To rid my soul of one dark blot;
> To Thee whose blood can cleanse each spot,
> O Lamb of God, I come, I come!

Just as I am, though tossed about
With many a conflict, many a doubt;
Fightings within, and fears without,
O Lamb of God, I come, I come!

79

Holier Than Thou

☙❧

Oh, isn't this the attitude we all dislike in others? That smug display of moral superiority from the intolerant. This is the "I am better than you are" chant that we heard as "My dad is stronger/faster/makes more money than your dad" when we were kids.

But we are all grown up now, so the mantra now is largely unspoken, but the comparisons are made in private circles and in families. Our house is bigger than theirs. We have much better taste than they do. Where do they shop, the thrift store? Our car is newer. We have the latest smartphones.

Think that is any different? We measure everything. It is how we help our egos to feel better than they would otherwise. Our human ego. That part of us that seems to need bolstering constantly. In our material world, our egos feel best when it considers itself better than the people that surround it. Better than people, cars, buildings, clothing, you name it.

Materialism. The strong focus, and often the irresistible desire, for tangible things, and the accumulation of wealth. Physical comfort at the top of our avaricious list of absolute necessities.

The world has given us great scientific and technological gifts that make us feel powerful. Sometimes, however, our ego, coupled with control and money get in the way of us truly finding happiness. Society convinces us to be prideful and class conscious, and we can get caught up in it all. To then measure ourselves by how much we possess is counter intuitive to the spiritual life we say we want.

Materialistic goals do not often leave much room for those inner values. Once our ego gets engaged, it is not the easiest task to free ourselves from the allure to please it.

Inadvertently, we can easily put on some righteous indignation by convincing ourselves that we have our egos in check. Then we can laud over others that we are better than those holier-than-thou folks because we put our spirituality, compassion and forgiveness first in our lives. We have greater virtue!! Well that is pretty self-righteous, don't you think? I would say that is just the other side of the same coin. It is no wonder that the Bible teaches us that God does not measure us by our works, let alone our own boasting.

Any smugness is wide off the mark. So, let us give up all the measuring, and the sanctimonious crap. You know what I think that all is? It's fear. Fear that we are not good enough, so we are trying to prove to the outside world that we are good enough because we have stuff, and lots of it. And if we do not have stuff, then our ego willingly decides that we are better than the next guy because we go to church more, we tithe more, or we are just plain holier than the next guy.

Why don't we all take a deep breath here? This ego trip is quite something. So let us back up a bit.

The fear that we are not enough is the opposite of love. Fear prevents love from entering. It keeps us frozen and all locked up inside. For love to flourish in our lives, we need to go with the flow of life. We need to let go of the unpleasant emotion of fear and stay open to what life offers. To what God offers us.

We do not have to point out that someone else is ignorant, for us to be wise. Nor do we have to acknowledge another's weaknesses to prove our strength. We do not have to try to kill our ego either. It is a part of our humanness.

Our egos will thrive when we grow personally, show passion, and creativity, and they will flourish as we expand our individuality. As we open up to possibility, we can stop quantifying everything and live in the moment. The joy of expressing gratitude and true forgiveness will become so compelling that we can learn to release all the control which, in the past, we were unable to live without. Wonderful and new experiences can bring real joy into our lives as we open the door to love, peace and understanding.

The love of God is not divisive. He does not exclude the weak or the insignificant. He includes them in His love. It is not who we are affiliated with that causes God to love us. It is not because we are better or worse than anyone else. He loves each of us the same. Nobody is better. When we show kindness, it is not to make God love us or love us more. Rather it is because we are demonstrating who we have become.

When we are open to receiving all the love that God has to offer, we do not need the fear in our lives anymore. Because we have finally learned that we are enough for Him. And He is all that matters. Do not try to be holy or righteous. Be yourself. Be real. Just listen to *The Velveteen Rabbit*.[27]

"He said, "You become. It takes a long time. That's why it doesn't happen often to people who break easily, or have sharp edges, or who have to be carefully kept. Generally, by the time you are Real, most of your hair has been loved off, and your eyes drop out and you get loose in the joints and very shabby. But these things don't matter at all, because once you are Real you can't be ugly, except to people who don't understand."

80

Bible Warfare

ೋ ೋ

Believers and non-believers alike love to get into discussions about the Bible. Some to say it is the absolute word of God, while others proclaim it is simply a work of fiction. Either way, the Bible has been battled over consistently through time. What makes us want to fight its contents so much?

Certainly, the Bible has made an impression in our world. It is the book most bought and distributed on the planet with more than five billion copies sold. Almost enough for each one of us to have one.

But what are the reasons to debate so much about its origin, its characters, history, and to question the truth behind it? What is our fascination? Are we experts in archaeology, and want to quarrel about where the Garden of Eden was located exactly? Are we historians disagreeing on the locations of the twelve ancient wars or the conflicts that caused the twenty plus battles in the Bible? Or are we the scholars of literature who long to disagree about the complications of putting so many differing stories together into one tome? Possibly we are mostly God-loving individuals fascinated by this gift we were given, and just want to find out the truth behind it?

Perhaps it is even simpler than that. Though we want to be correct in our own thinking, we end up pushing our thoughts onto others. Some Bible battlers are genuinely interested in understanding the word of God. Yet that does not ease their demeanor nor their desire to prove a point.

When we are debating strongly on a topic so close to our hearts, we believe that our strong faith could not possibly be misinterpreted or lead us astray. So we insist that our information is absolutely factual.

God: no God. Proof: no proof of a man named Jesus. Men who lived for centuries. Ninety-year-old women giving birth. Creation. Revelation. Oh, there is so much to ponder and fight over. Not to mention the twentieth century discoveries of two-thousand-year-old scrolls from the Dead Sea.

Shall we add some fuel to the fire? This too is from the Bible. The Bible has unicorns. Fortune telling and astrology is not forbidden. The Bible never promises us that God will not give us more than we can handle. And there is plenty in the Bible about owning slaves and animal sacrifices.

So, what do we do with those parts? Should we fight over whose interpretation of the Bible is correct, or should we allow our own personal faith to guide us. It is religion we argue about, the dogma.

We cannot be afraid to learn something new, even about the Good Book. It is a test of our faith to have challenges. Those challenges should never change the way we feel about our God. There will always be opposition.

Perhaps the simple question to ask is: do we have a religion, or do we have faith?

We can be strong in our faith, yet open to acquiring new experiences in our conviction. Our faith is what touches our hearts and can be displayed in the most fruitful ways.

Our faith can know no bounds. The conviction we feel is strident. We cannot allow differences to be what we are about, while at the same time claiming to want to celebrate and share the love of God. We must use our deep faith to move from dissent to acceptance, and from divisiveness to inclusiveness.

Let us release the desire to be right, let alone argue about this sin being bigger than that sin. Let us move towards the love that most of us agree God is all about. Let us turn the Bible wars into love in action.

Let us demonstrate our deep care for the less fortunate, the poor, and those weaker in body and spirit. Let us practice loving someone who is difficult to love and forgive another who has wronged us. Let us reach out past those we are close to and have much in common with, to share God's love out in the world. May we reach past judging those who are unlike us.

May we learn to make giving and sharing a part of our devotion to Him. The simplest gift can be the most loving gesture. A smile. A helping hand when needed. Food for the hungry. Oh so many people go hungry each day. Donations of any kind.

Verily I say unto you, Inasmuch as ye have done it unto one of the least of these my brethren, ye have done it unto me. *(Matthew 25:40 KJV)*

81

Spring Cleaning

☙❧

Winter in the Northeast United States where I grew up, was never a picnic in the park. It was more of a hibernation of all creatures great and small. Cold. Gray. Snow. That wintery mix that was impossible to deal with. Rinse and repeat, over and over for months. But come March and certainly April, and the promise of spring became a longing we felt in our bodies and minds. A longing to again feel the warmth of the sun on our faces and in our fingertips. No longer the need for gloves or a buttoned-up jacket. Hats and scarves now destined to be left behind when it got too warm for them to be needed. So, we dropped them on the spot when the sun brightened up.

Spring. The long dormant earth awakens. Spikey naked tree branches suddenly tipped with green. Crocus breaking through the now unfrozen soil. A sweetness wafts on soft breezes. Warmth is provided from the sun and now the Earth as well. Our windows are flung open to let in the clean fresh air, and the staleness from being closed up for months, vanishes. And finally, we can start to plan those picnics in the park.

As the earth gets ready for its new beginning, so do we. We do much more than just freshen up our gardens, and our homes for the wondrous days to come when light will fill our mornings, and then stay around for long evening hours. We Spring clean!

This annual tradition means that every inch of the garden is to be cleared of the weeds and debris that accumulated during the winter months. Plants are cut back, encouraging new growth and renewal, and we prepare the soil for the upcoming growth season by adding in some organic matter. We set up the new planter beds envisioned last year. We browse seed catalogs and look forward to nursery visits where the little pots of fresh herbs show up first. We pull out all the garden tools and clean them up for the new season.

In the home the windows are cleaned inside and out to sparkling brightness. All the curtains come down for a good washing; every drapery sent out for dry cleaning. Blinds and shutters have every nook and cranny wiped clean. Each corner is emptied of clutter and dust, and every molding, top and bottom, practically spit-shined. Fresh bed linens smell especially sweet once the mattresses have been aired out. And the closets? We clean them out as well, donating the winter clothes we never wore, and putting the brightly colored items in the front.

Yes, spring cleaning means getting a fresh start. We dread all of the work needed to get it done, but we love the outcome.

What about our Soul Gardens? Couldn't they use some freshening up for spring? This is something we may hold deeply inside: A desire to change some of our thinking or some of our actions. Now is a great time to plan our soul garden's growth.

Every great garden should have a plan. What is it that we would like to accomplish? We are all different, and our lists will be different as well. For example, perhaps we would like to become a kinder and gentler person. Or maybe we would like to have an open mind and heart. Wonderful goals, no matter where we currently are on the path.

How then do we accomplish these objectives for our soul garden? Let us first set our intentions. We have stated our goals in general, so now, let us be more specific.

Be kinder. To whom do we want to show kindness? In what situations would we like ourselves to be more caring and empathetic? The more specific, the more we can focus in on the how.

Be more open with our heart and mind...Again, details are essential. Perhaps we would like to stop fear from keeping us from new experiences and beliefs. Or, we would like to be more open to the spiritual opinions of others? Perhaps there is someone that we have in mind.

The magic to accomplishing our goals can be that we be present in our lives. Some say it is being in the moment or being mindful. Be here now. Living one's life in the present is a full-time job. It takes practice, and often some hard work. One way to be truly present is to let go of the past. Now that does not mean to drop all hurt and frustration without doing the emotional work needed to clear the pain of the past. Doing that work will help us to live our lives in the present.

Ask God for His guidance on the journey. Thank Him for His love. Seek His counsel. Then, with His help, when we plant the seeds we desire for our soul growth; the seeds of compassion, forgiveness, and love, we can have the confidence that they will take root.

Cultivate those seeds. How to do that? Live in the moment. We must catch ourselves as often as we can to come back into the present. Being in the moment is what nurtures those beautiful seeds, because it means our minds, our bodies, and our souls are focused. That brings our attention, thoughts, and feelings into the present as well.

The difficult part of remaining present is that we all carry different types of baggage with us. Memories, resentments, emotional stress, and we all seem to enjoy making old hurts a part of our current life. To move forward, we must surrender to our humanness, and mindfulness will help greatly with that as well. Affirmations help but do take the time to take the affirmation to heart, believing the statement is true now, in the present. Bring the goodness of what you want and what you dream into your present life. Behave as though all you have prayed for has already been granted.

Spring cleaning is all about nurturing ourselves and manifesting our desires. After all we are tending to seeds that we want to have flourish under our care. Staying mindful helps us to be kinder and more caring. It aids us in being open to what others are going through. Being present helps us to open our minds and our hearts to the truth of what is happening around us. We can then choose our reaction and monitor more closely what we say. Never forget that what is happening is Divine and that every moment of our lives is holy.

Once we master mindfulness, the seeds of compassion, forgiveness, and love will bloom. We will find our authentic selves in the blossoming of our own soul, all from a few beautiful seeds we planted in our hearts and minds.

82

Peace

☙❦

It is what we pray for. It is what we say we long for in this world. But will it ever show up in our lives? And if it does, will we recognize it?

As I grew up and learned about all the wars that seemed endless, I had to wonder if this unsettled world was just the way it had to be. As a species we have some magnificent traits and extraordinary abilities, but we also come with a few characteristics that are both alarming and frightening. Anger and hatred for sure. My conclusion was that as human beings, we could not get away from war. It felt that there would always be at least one war going on every day in this world. I read that the Tibetans had tried but were easily overrun. Those who wanted to live in peace needed protectors to be sure. Were there enough of those around? I had to wonder.

Peace has various definitions depending on whom you ask. Some consider it the absence of war, while others define it as serenity or even inner peace. For most of us, having peace in our lives, even for a moment, is a good thing.

Politics and religion have never been good conversational material. Those topics start battles between the best of friends and the most beloved relatives. Yet these subjects seem to share one more thing lately. Rather than strive to include others, they strive for divisiveness.

It feels that we enjoy getting caught up in and arguing about most anything. People kick and scream to get ahead for money, power, and to climb corporate ladders. We defend our thoughts and opinions as if a life depended on it. And not on subjects where a life is truly at stake. We fight for what is right, and what we think is right at the time. We debate and dispute. We quarrel and squabble. Are confrontations and wars supposed to provide fulfillment and satisfaction?

There is a peace and calmness that life offers if we choose to pursue it. The depth and breadth of our addiction to life's distractions are our own. And each of us must find our own method of withdrawal. We need to find our willingness and enthusiasm for the stillness. Therein lie our hearts and souls, just the way God made us. Meditation and prayer are not only great steps in achieving some quiet time for the mind, but they are also the pathway to discovering serenity in the silence.

We must endeavor to place the peace of God at the center of our being and allow that peace to radiate outward into the rest of our lives. It can touch all aspects of our being, our friendships, relatives, work, community, and the world. We just have to allow it to do so.

This takes work, but so does anything that is worthwhile. Solitude and inner peace are well worth it. There is a harmony in accepting who we are, and that God loves us unconditionally. This will go a long way toward ending the inner struggles...and we all have inner struggles.

The peace we crave is not a competition. It is a gift that is sincerely possible for us to attain, and one we must learn to accept. This yearning we feel is for a peacefulness that will make our souls sing.

Let us strive to not be prisoners to our own fear, anger, and bitterness. What fight is worth that? Do we want to be right or do we want to be happy?

It is in the stillness that we can find our waiting Lord. Which of the trials or burdens that we bear can be carried to the Prince of Peace, and laid at His feet? Perhaps we have forgotten that we can do that. There is comfort there. Find and accept His peace. Recognize its presence. Accept it, and keep it in your heart and in your mind. Feel it with your whole heart, then share it. The peace that He offers to us is really what we are seeking.

83

Surrounded

ഗ്രര

Did your mother ever tell you that she just did not like that other kid you started hanging around with? Did you understand at the time what the fuss was all about? Mom understood. What you surround yourself with is what you become.

We must make so very many choices in this amazing life of ours. Now while we may believe we do not select our parents and families. Consider everything else. Where we choose to live. The type of work we do. Our spouse. Our friends. Whether to go to college or not, and where that might be located. The religion we follow or don't. And the music we listen to. All choices. Decisions we make for our lives.

And each one of those preferences we opted for or against, would change the world we are surrounded by every day. Each country on the planet has a different ambiance. And each city and state in America is distinctive, and not just in geography. There are varying levels of acceptance whether it be religion, lifestyle, availability of cultural activities and so forth. Each creates a unique atmosphere for its populaces.

Challenging work and an environment where I am safe and protected are my choices. Cosmopolitan vibes make me happy. Your choices may be similar or very different. But we can each surround ourselves with what pleases us. That is a type of freedom that is priceless.

Surrounding ourselves with the choices we have made should be comforting. But the question of the day is, are those the selections the best ones for us? Not every decision always plays out exactly the way we hope and plan.

When we are surrounded, we are enclosed on all sides. Every part of our being is exposed to the atmosphere we have created. The good and the bad. Therefore, every lyric we sing, the personalities of each of our friends, every attribute of society we emulate, creates the environment in which we thrive or in which we do not.

Sometimes change is needed when the ambience is just not healthy or productive. Those alterations are not always the easiest to carry out. But they may be necessary to elicit the future we desire.

Do we think to envelope ourselves in the grace and love of God? Choosing that daily and thanking Him for His love and guidance will get us going in the right direction. Pray for protection and the strength to carry on. Thank Him for all of the blessings. Invoke His assistance with all the choices and decisions, as well as any changes that need to be made. Who better to have on our side?

84

Tithes and Offerings

☙❧

Yes, money. It is currency that dominates our culture. It is a part of our holy life as well, as we are raised to believe that tithes and offerings support the work of the Lord. We have been known to call money the 'almighty dollar.' It is not uncommon to know people who worship money, are obsessed with it, and for whom material possessions are the essence of their existence. They pursue fame and fortune as a means of finding their place in this world. They do not even realize that true satisfaction and joy does not reside there.

Churchgoers offer money to our houses of worship. Some to impress, but others because of the belief that everything we have is ultimately a gift from God, and this is a way to demonstrate that we recognize Him as the Lord of our lives.

God may love each of us the very same, but in following Him, does that make us want to offer Him more than a few dollars in that offering plate? If we truly believe that the Lord has provided blessings to us, blessings like waking up each morning, breathing, having family and friends, being loved. Don't we want to offer Him something of ourselves? The more we accept life as a beautiful gift from God, the more joy we can experience and share.

So how do we offer our experience of God's blessings to the world? We give more than just money. We contribute to our world through participating in it with the same joy and love we get from God.

We offer kindness and generosity. We say 'thank you' every time a door is held open or change is given. After all, isn't a 'thank you' the very simplest of gestures? And is that not what we say to the Lord at the beginning and end of every day?

We offer compassion with a 'God Bless You' to a stranger now and again. And we say it to our loved ones without a sneeze being involved. We do not leave off the God and just said 'bless you' either. We take every opportunity to reflect and share the love we have in our hearts for the God that gave us life.

We show integrity in all that we do, and we are honest with every transaction. We ask ourselves where we show our humanity the most, and the least, and we adjust that as needed. We also reflect on who gets the benefit of our compassion and amend that as well.

An offering is a donation, a gift. Each of our remaining days could be a tribute to the Lord we say we believe in and love with all our heart and with all our mind. This goes way beyond just money on an offering plate.

We do not all have money to give, but we have 'thank you's' to voice and integrity to demonstrate. There is humility to reveal, and generosity that can be provided without ready cash. In fact, the only thing we may have to offer to the Lord is the true love in our hearts, and perhaps, that is all He ever wanted.

85

Here and Now

☙❧

It is Palm Sunday today. And it is good for us to remember what makes this such a special day for Christians, and how events will play out in the week to come.

This trip that Jesus took into Jerusalem, came after He had traveled many months on His path of preaching and healing. Palm Sunday is a celebration of Jesus' triumphal entry into Jerusalem. It is said that Jesus was going to claim His title as the Messiah: The Messiah that God had promised in an ancient prophecy from the Old Testament. Jesus rode this path into Jerusalem on a donkey: the donkey symbolizing that He was coming in peace. The people waved palm branches and praised Jesus with Hosannas. Hosanna being an expression of adoration, of praise, and of joy.

How this title of Messiah was to be bestowed on Him by all the peoples, we will never know...

Palm Sunday was always a favorite of mine when I was a child. Spring had sprung, and the chatter after church services was lively and outdoors in newly warmer weather. The palm fronds with their gentle, tropical smell were a welcome sign of spring after a long winter. However, I must say that I never really had any idea of what was to come for my friend Jesus in this week ahead. Children just follow along with the same Bible stories that came up every so often.

Palm Sunday is the beginning of Holy Week.[28] In a few days, Jesus will celebrate Passover with His disciples, setting Himself on His new path toward crucifixion. It is believed that Jesus and His disciples spent much of this Holy week with His good friend, Lazarus and his family in Bethany.

Monday brings us the money changers at the temple, where Jesus announces that the temple should be a house of prayer and overturns the tables of the merchants. From then and into the next day, there is much discussion amongst the rabbis, for you see, Jesus' actions were like a proclamation of His being a spiritual authority in the temple. The religious leaders decided to arrest Jesus but became afraid of the crowds who supported Him.

Later this same day, Tuesday, Jesus left Jerusalem for the Mount of Olives with four of his Apostles, and spoke to them about the destruction of Jerusalem, and what was to come. This day is also the day that Judas Iscariot made a deal with the Sanhedrin.

Thursday brought the Passover feast. Jesus shared much with His disciples about loving one another during the supper, and He washed their feet. He spoke to them of His suffering to come; yet another indication that Jesus knew the path He was on. Jesus led the group in the Lord's Supper, instructing them to always remember His sacrifice by sharing bread and wine.

It was in the Garden of Gethsemane later that same night where Jesus prayed to the Father. During that prayer, His sweat became drops of blood. It was here that Jesus was betrayed by the kiss of Judas and was arrested by the Sanhedrin.

Jesus' crimes were that He healed people on the Sabbath, created havoc in the temple, and claimed to be the Son of God. So serious were these crimes that He was brought immediately to the home of Caiaphas, the High Priest. Joseph Caiaphas was the most powerful religious authority in Judea, and a known enemy of Jesus. The ruling rabbis felt Jesus was incredibly dangerous, and urged Caiaphas to send Him to Pontius Pilate, the Roman governor, who had the power to condemn someone to death. Not that Pilate would have cared about the blasphemy, but the Sanhedrin purposefully accused Jesus of treason so that He could be condemned by the Romans.

Pilate, however, was reluctant at first, to carry out the task of condemnation. He did not want to comply with the Jewish demand. Pilate knew that Herod Antipas, the ruler of Galilee, was spending a few days in Jerusalem at the time, and sent Jesus over to him. Herod and his soldiers treated Jesus with contempt, throwing beautiful robes on Him and taunting this supposed King of the Jews. They mocked Him, and then sent him back to Pilate.

Once back in the hands of Pilate, Jesus was convicted of treason and of declaring Himself to be the King of the Jews. Pilate had Jesus crucified the same day. Jesus was ridiculed and beaten. He was then forced to carry His own cross to Calvary, where He was nailed to it and put on display. Crucifixion is inconceivably cruel.

These stories are modified for children in Sunday School. Though we are taught the 'story,' the idea of these events being physically painful is muffled intentionally. The idea seems to be to move us on to the great event and celebration of the resurrection. But as we grow up and understand the torture and the viciousness that was exhibited there, it is impossible in the here and now to go through Holy Week without the greatest sense of sorrow and grief. The wretchedness, and the plight of a people that offered such intense cruelty as a response to love and healing.

Jesus spoke from the cross. Some of His words asked that the Father forgive His persecutors, because they had no idea what they were doing. In the end, Jesus committed his spirit to our Father in heaven.

The body of Jesus was taken down and laid in a tomb owned by Joseph of Arimathea. Both Joseph of Arimathea and Nicodemus were members of the Sanhedrin, the very court that had condemned Jesus. Yet both men lived in secret as followers of Jesus. It was they who cared for the body of Jesus and prepared it for burial with spices and oils. His body was guarded by Roman soldiers through the next day.

In reverence to this day, Palm Sunday, and to this Holy Week, perhaps we should ask ourselves, where are we today on our own paths? Do we know where we are headed? Do we live in the here and now, or do we live somewhere in the past or in the hope of the future?

We tend to think of paths as roads to a successful life or career, yet there are also paths to righteousness and spirituality. The path to anywhere requires at least some introspection and decision making. And paths are not always straight nor are they the easiest way to get somewhere. Often the pathway is littered with rocks and stones, or even boulders. Frequently there are rivers to ford not knowing where the path will pick up on the other side. Sometimes we are swept away or forced to navigate impossibly slick rocks. But as they say, it is the journey. Our singular journey.

As we continue to learn about and travel our own paths to find our place in the world, we should remember that we all waiver sometimes. We even completely lose our way occasionally, but it is all okay. We would be blessed to remember that every moment is holy and that the grace and the unending love of God is all around us no matter where we are on life's pathway.

Whatever your story may be. Whatever your path. It is yours and yours alone. Just consider the possibilities though, if one day you hear your Lord say to you, "Follow My path."

86

Oh, Happy Day!

৪০ ৫৪

Amost joyous and blessed Resurrection morning to you. This glorious day of celebration is our oldest holiday, and the most important event on the Christian calendar. Our belief as Christians is that our Lord has risen today, and He lives! This Easter Sunday is the basis of our faith.

My large chocolate bunny is by my side, and sadly no eggs were dyed for the customary egg wars. But the memories are alive still.

Today we reach the culmination of Holy Week, and what a week it was. The world almost lost the whole of the 856 year-old Paris Notre Dame Cathedral on Monday, and this week the Vatican decided to uncover the steps that Jesus climbed to be judged by Pilate, hidden for 300 years.

The Notre Dame Cathedral stood through war and revolution. She has needed multiple restorations through the years, due not only to hundreds of years of wear and tear, but the elements and acid rain have also taken a severe toll. And there were the years of neglect and for some decades now, thousands of tourists each day.

In the long history, the church bells were melted down to make cannons, and statues of kings were removed and beheaded in the public squares. If only those porticos could talk.

Before the fire the Cathedral was again in a state of disrepair. Decorative cement was being replaced with plywood, and the gargoyles didn't even look scary anymore. Notre-Dame is now facing the largest restoration since the mid-eighteen hundreds. Within days more than one billion Euro were pledged for her restoration.

I fell in love with Notre-Dame de Paris the moment I laid eyes on her from across the Seine. Taking in every inch of that Gothic masterpiece with her flying buttresses and bell towers, it felt like history came alive to me for the first time. The beauty and elegance of Notre-Dame, and all she had witnessed since her beginnings in 1163, overwhelm me. And I have been known to hug her interior columns.

From Vatican City, the announcement came this week that the holy stairs will be revealed to the public this spring after being covered for 300 years. The holy stairs are those that Jesus climbed and descended many times on His way to judgment by Pontius Pilate. The stairs are stained by three drops of Jesus's blood.

In a short few days, the world lost much of an irreplaceable religious icon in Notre-Dame de Paris and gained knowledge of another significant relic of Christianity in the holy stairs. Will this renew the conviction of the faithful and open the possibility of belief to those who are yet to find comfort in Him?

Occasionally it takes tragedy to find Him. Sometimes it takes a new door opening to an old staircase. Are they not both proof that rebirth and resurrection are real?

This resurrection day brings a familiar song to mind... "Oh Happy Day."[29]

> Happy day, (oh happy day)
> When Jesus washed, (when Jesus washed)
> When Jesus washed, (when Jesus washed)
> Jesus washed, (when Jesus washed)
> Washed my sins away (oh happy day)
> Oh happy day, (oh happy day)

Oh happy day, (oh happy day)
Oh happy day, (oh happy day)
When Jesus washed, (when Jesus washed)
When Jesus washed, (when Jesus washed)
When my Jesus washed, (when Jesus washed)
Washed my sins away

He taught me how (oh taught me how)
To watch, (to watch)
Fight and pray (to fight and pray), fight and pray
(and taught me how and live rejoicing)
And live rejoicing every, every day, every day

Oh happy day, (oh happy day)
Oh happy day, (oh happy day)
Jesus washed, (when Jesus washed)
When Jesus washed, (when Jesus washed)
When Jesus washed, (when Jesus washed)
My sins away (oh happy day)
And taught each other happy day (oh happy day)

He taught me how (he taught me how, how)
To watch, (to watch)
Fight and pray (sing, sing, come on and sing),
Fight and pray
(and till me, yeah, yeah, come on everybody)
And live rejoicing every, every day, every day
And live rejoicing every, every day,
(sing like me, yeah) everyday

Oh happy day, (oh happy day)
Oh happy day, (oh happy day)
Oh happy day, (oh happy day)
Oh happy day, (oh happy day)

87

God Did It

☙❧

Good or bad. Right or wrong. Whatever happens: God did it. Seems it is either 'Thanks be to God' or it is 'Why me, Lord?' If we are unhappy with life's circumstances or do not get what we want, we blame God. We may think God is angry with us, and some religions actually teach that God gets mad at His children. Or the opposite happens, and we get angry with God, and when circumstances do not change for the better, many turn away from Him completely.

We are taught that God is omnipotent. So, we question why He would let bad things happen to His children, created in His image. We are taught that God is loving: How could a loving God let disease, murder, poverty, and homelessness happen? We are taught that God is our Father in heaven. But why does life sometimes feel so cruel?

We are taught that God is the King of Kings. That all things were possible, if only we believe in Him. And we learn that faith as small as a tiny mustard seed, would allow us to move mountains.

Right now, I have friends struggling with their faith for many reasons. They are grappling with the promises that living in faith gave them. They honored their parents and hoped to live long lives with the blessings the Lord had for them. They have hopes that the Lord will renew their strength. They believed the Lord when he told them not to fear, that He would help them. They have prayed over their children, their marriages, and their loved ones. They would never complete a business deal without first running it past their Lord and Savior. And yet disease and tragedies have found them.

Now they feel lost and alone, and try not to be mad at God, yet wonder if He is angry with them. It is hard times when you feel that the promises of the God you believe in are not coming through the way you want them to, nor the way you expected they would.

Often this struggle leads to us to question our faith. This type of spiritual experience is a life-shaking, life-changing time of sadness, depression, grief, and/or emotional challenge. Profound changes in life can happen because of these episodes of disbelief. The experience can be deeply symbolic, and it can turn one's life and belief system upside down. The experience can bring about a new phase in one's life, and its occurrence is as individual as each person going through it.

Faith is more than just a belief that God exists or a hope that He does. Faith connects us to God and makes Him real. Faith needs trust.

Trust is basic to human relationships. Being able to trust means we know someone well enough to be able to predict what they will do in a situation. Trusting in the Lord is about heartfelt knowing that as our Father, he loves us unconditionally, and only wants the very best for us. It is about accepting that our Father may allow us to experience things on this Earth, so that we may grow into our full potential. We do not know what our lives will be like in the future, but He does.

Experiencing life with God at our center does not mean that life is perfect, that our families are faultless, or that we will never suffer any loss or encounter any challenge that we cannot overcome. It means we will experience all that life has to offer, both the suffering and the joy, and we will know God through each encounter.

We may be having these experiences to further our own spiritual healing or spiritual growth. Or we may be being used as an example of how a faithful servant responds.

Imagine the perfect Father. Always loving. Always guiding. Always present. Always knowing what is best for us. Practice faith. Give trust a chance.

While it is true I have not moved any mountains yet, I am still trying...

88

Providence

⁂

Each and every one of us is in the protective care of God. This is a very comforting thought, and there is no place else I would rather be. Is this thought provoking or just another type of affirmation that the mind accepts and moves on from? What if we took the time to contemplate this?

In order to reflect on anything, we must calm our minds and focus on it. Until we form the habit, we may find it difficult or nearly impossible to shut out all the 'to do's' and daily pressures we feel. We may want to blame the path of civilization or technological progress, but our daily lives have always demanded our attention. The volume of elements that are calling to us has risen dramatically in the past decades, and if electronic devices are involved, we are advised that their overuse and abuse is an addiction. We have even trained ourselves to expect and to enjoy excessive mental stimulation and activity. Whatever the dependence or compulsion may be, we need to resolve it for our health and sanity.

We would love to assume that the distractions claiming our focus are not only positive in nature but are also things more wonderful than the rest of our lives. Not so. Have you ever noticed that our focus just loves to go toward the negative; whether it is for the purpose of survival, or just the feeling of relief we sometimes get. But the positive affirmations and meditations are, for most of us, a real struggle to maintain.

What would be best is to find 'me' time in the hustle and bustle of life, but also to find some genuine quietude. We say we want peace and quiet, yet we do not always know what to do with it, should we find some. In fact many of us cannot enjoy the stillness. Our personalities just cannot deal with silence and tranquility. So, we are always on the phone, on social media, always interacting with someone or something.

When we want to think about God's blessings, for example, we need to think profoundly which requires freedom from distractions. It does require peacefulness to be able to focus and consider the magnitude of something like providence. With practice, silence is a joy, and something we look forward to having it in our lives. It is amazingly addictive.

Getting to that peaceful place involves patience and practice. Try some prayer or meditation in the outdoors or while listening to music. Being quiet enough to listen to nature is rewarding in itself. Hearing the birds, insects, or water flowing somewhere is very peaceful. The sounds of nature can be quite intoxicating.

Centering our thoughts on God can lead to a peaceful state of mind. Consider how overwhelmingly loving He is. It is the immenseness of this subject that allows the mind to relax while being in awe of the universe that He created. Peaceful stillness is a beautiful state of mind.

Now that we have found the solitude and peacefulness, what do with do with the vision of being in God's protective care? Stay on the thought and go with it. Contemplate how it makes you feel and how amazing it is to feel that loved. Tears may flow as we experience being closely in touch with that much love.

This type of quiet time and thoughtful contemplation is good for the soul. It brings a peaceful calmness to us as it reveals our essence. It is good for the body too, as the release of stress is a byproduct of this meditative prayer. It lowers the blood pressure and allows us to relieve all the tensions that have built up. It is also something the Bible reminds us to do: Be still, and know that I am God. *(Psalms 46:10 KJV)*

89

Seeing With Spiritual Eyes

※

Start off by feeling calm and grateful, the way we would want to start out every single day. Feel safe in your surroundings and create the desire to look and feel with an open heart and an open mind. Look with love onto the magical world we live in.

Muster up all our feelings of compassion, of patience and forgiveness that we have ever felt, and realize that everyone we know is on their own path in this life, and that is okay. We must, therefore, be free of judgement when we consider other's lives and their choices of how to live in this world. Because everything happens for each person in the right way and at the right time. And though their belief systems are different from our own, we do not need to, nor do we have a desire to judge. We will not judge because we know that judging the lives, actions or beliefs of others really means we are determining their worthiness to have and receive love. And we know that judging others pushes us away from God. We also know that God is loving and comes with open arms for everyone.

We will not often understand why things happen the

way they do, so we step back into an observational point of view when we lack understanding of what we see. And we do our best to feel a sense of unconditional love and understanding that we are all in different places in life at this moment.

We can try to see the Light of God in each person we know, and do our best to treat them as if that is the only thing we see in them. And we can try to understand the concept that there is no right and no wrong. Just a different path to take.

Perhaps we can lovingly look at that which resonates deeply within ourselves? Our vulnerabilities. Our anger. Our passions. And we can decide to look at those conditions more closely and with the same unconditional love we want to offer others but can now offer it to ourselves. Our frailties are just as much a part of us as our strengths and our courage. Our shortcomings exist as do our many powers, though we are inclined to ignore anything we do not perceive as positive in nature.

So we shall focus on the power of love, and see that in our world. Love leads us to peace, and joy, and freedom from judgement. Love can help us change our focus to one of connection rather than divisiveness. Connection to the earth, to the universe, to God, and to each other.

Love leads the way to gratitude. May we be so very grateful each and every day that we are never again without the genuine appreciation for all that life has given us.

Gratitude leads us to prayer. May we pray so abundantly that each day becomes a prayer of thankfulness for the enormous blessing of having this precious life. Recognizing the blessing becomes the need to convey that same blessing on others that they may receive only the very best from this life and feel blessed themselves.

Beyond that, we desire to love God more today than yesterday. By loving Him more, we open ourselves to love everything about life more deeply than we ever imagined was possible. In any situation, we find ourselves being kinder, because it is bubbling up joyously from the core of our being. We begin experiencing a deeper empathy than we knew we had. We even show that compassion to ourselves and learn to forgive that which we previously could not.

We become the miracle instead of waiting for one to appear.

90

Choosing to Live with a Spiritual Heart

❧☙

Heaven may be our home, but we do not live there quite yet. We do live on a planet with an overflowing quantity of issues that are a part of dwelling with multitudes of humans of many races, numerous religions, oodles of personalities, and countless opinions.

Many of us try our very best to live a somewhat Godly life. Yet we realize with almost every challenge we face that we are imperfect humans. We stumble on the blurred lines of society that seem to barricade us from living our lives at times, over issues that others bulldoze right through. That may be society's challenge but living with a spiritually open heart can often feel like an arduous task.

We would like to think that to most questions, and all arguments, love is invariably the answer. So, we will begin, and optimistically we shall end, with love. We try to do our best, but find love is easiest from afar and in generalities. Where we tend to struggle is with up close and personal love. The kind of love that Jesus was so good at.

Love is affection and friendship. Love is tenderness and fondness. Love is what opens the human heart to a new way of experiencing the world. Love is what the Lord provides in every aspect of our being, and what we give back to Him with devotion and worship.

Let us look at our life's experience for a bit. Have we felt unconditional love from a parent, or we have felt it for a child for whom all our love spilled out uncontrollably? Have we experienced an incredibly loving partner? Maybe we have had a dog as a best friend who showered us with unconditional love, and we felt the same way in return.

Have we ever felt love so deeply that we just cannot explain what it feels like to our friends? Maybe we have been to a place so beautiful that it seemed to be utterly indescribable, and it resonated with us deeply?

Or, have we ever known someone who was different or unusual? Challenged or disabled in some way perhaps, yet they have the most beautiful outlook and loving personality. A person we cannot help but love because we can see and feel the infinite beauty of the love that person brings to life, and their joy is screaming so loudly, that we just cannot resist.

Have we ever loved someone who got very sick or who passed on, and found ourselves willing to take their place rather than contemplating the thought of losing them?

These are just some experiences that demonstrate to us the expanded version of what love truly is if we allow it to show itself. That love we feel with the whole of our being, taken into our hearts, and allowed it to magnify our experience and our compassion along with it.

This is what a spiritual heart is. It is a love which expands the boundaries of everything that we are, into what we could become. This sensation becomes such a remarkable part of us that we will never ever forget what it feels like. Unrestrained love is overwhelming to humans. We feel it with every sense, and we are overloaded with the emotion. It is the awareness of pure joy. It is immeasurable ecstasy, and leaves most of us sobbing.

Love makes us better. Love is why we stand up to intolerance and lack of empathy. Love for humanity is why we insist the world show no tolerance towards the many violations of human rights that we see in the world. Love is why we cherish each other and care about the world.

Let us remember all our loving experiences. Especially the ones that bring us to our knees, for it is there that we will find our true and spiritual hearts. Now we must choose to live with that feeling, that knowing, for every remaining day of our lives. For what we focus on in life is what we become.

91

Erring on the Side of Love

☙☜

The English poet, Alexander Pope, gave us the proverb, "To err is human, to forgive divine." Preachers of all denominations tell us that we are all sinners. In fact, we cannot help but be such. We are born that way, apparently. Therefore, we will always err; blundering and stumbling our way through this life.

Mistakes. There is no sense pretending. We make them. From the whoops and the oops, to the defective judgment. From the misconceptions to the carelessness. Or perhaps on occasion we have failed to behave according to accepted standards.

It is the mistakes we make against each other with assumptions and judgments that are most concerning. Of course, we are human. It is part of our condition that we are protective of ourselves and the people we care about. So, we evaluate constantly to decide if a threat is present that we need to defend ourselves against. Should we feel in any way threatened, our arrogance may start to build out of fear. And if the threat increases, we may handle it by throwing out a bit of condescending behavior, in the hopes the other human will back down.

It could be we are having a lousy day, we are unsuccessfully dealing with great physical pain, or we have the emotional need to display superiority. Now our first thought may be, 'but I don't do that,' yet if one human is capable of 'doing that' then we all are. It is a possibility, not a guaranteed characteristic.

Not all humans come into this life surrounded by loving parents in a beautiful environment. Not all are tended to as the precious gifts from God that they are. And not all parents have the emotional proficiency to deal with the needs of a child, or a toddler, or a teenager. Many adults do not understand their own emotional needs, let alone are able to parent in a healthy and responsible way all the time. We all need help.

We need to grasp the healthy concept and the range of emotions that love is. We have different families and come from a variety of cultures. We have diverse upbringings. We follow dissimilar laws from both moral, societal, and religious foundations. Nonetheless, when we laugh and when we cry, it is the same.

As the faulty humans we are, most of us are eager, perhaps even desperate for the tenderness and affection of love. We want to feel it in our lives, and we want to joyously offer it to others. But we are very picky in determining who deserves our love, our attention, and our compassion.

Yet even love needs practice. Loving ourselves is of equal importance to loving others. The actions go hand in hand.

Love is the answer, but don't we need to deal with the question? Can we, in good conscience, talk about love without having a dialogue about hate? Perhaps being more loving should start with acknowledging what we do hate, and that we are taught to hate. We also need to recognize what we choose to hate.

We abhor those who are different and detest what we do not yet understand. Those feelings are potent, compelling, and intoxicating. There is no way we can resolve what we do not acknowledge exists, even if we know the answer.

Love is the joy and affection we crave, as well as the devotion and worship we long to give. It is the feeling and deep emotion that is gratifying to the spirit, bringing contentment to the soul. It is the kindness and patience shown to oneself and to others. It is that love which can conquer the hate in the world. Let us try to do that. Let us conquer hate. And if we are going to err anyway, shouldn't we err on the side of love?

92

Jesus or Nothing

☙❧

Jesus: the man, the prophet, the Messiah. Jesus, the whole reason behind Christianity. Is He the one we should worship or the one we should emulate? The ideas and answers change depending on who you ask.

Remember the 'Jesus Freaks' from the 1960's and 70's? Not a very kind name for people who were so very dedicated to Jesus that they spoke of nothing else. 'Bible Thumpers'... another disparaging name for folks longing to follow Him.

Did you know that originally it was an insult to be called a Christian? Yet now many say it proudly. Humans are a fickle bunch, aren't we?

We do not really talk about it much, except in critical accusations, but what does it take for us to accept another Christian or another believer in God from a different sect or a religion other than our own? It feels like it takes quite a lot. We don't talk about it because it is judgmental for us to do so.

So, what if some evangelical Christian youth enjoyed communal living? What if they enjoyed the fruits and lessons of not only Bible study, but the work of the Holy Spirit in their modern-day life. What if the hippies of the 'Jesus People' enjoyed the including meditation and Eastern religious practices? Who are we to say that what was in their hearts?

Many Christians seem to have deep seated fears about God, opinions on everything, and other's worthiness. Many are missing the whole point of grace. Instead we have very particular expectations of those who call themselves Christian, or anyone who claims to believe in and love the Lord.

Honestly, we cannot even decide if we should worship Jesus, emulate Him, or just argue about Him. Can man truly emulate the Son of God? If we would only admit how very confused we are.

We think we should be discerning about taking another Christian into our homes, or into our hearts. We judge others who are different...by what we think is right. We judge those who believe in God, but think Jesus is merely a prophet.

We disapprove of those who are unsure of what created this world. We assess negatively, the value of a person who follows a different path, even if that person lives a Godlier life than we do. By doing that we forget the simplest of His lessons.

So very many of us are not sure what is in our own hearts. How can we judge the hearts of others? The Bible states in *Matthew 5:8 (KJV)* that "Blessed are the pure in heart: for they shall see God." Seems we are just going to have to wait to find out, aren't we? I would love to see God... wouldn't you?

93

Why Now, Lord?

☙❧

Many of us labor over finding our purpose in life. And if we look at the turmoil in our world today, we are probably asking Him, not only why we are here, but also why is all this chaos happening now? We consistently see so much divisiveness and hate. Is it any wonder that more and more people are seeking to live off the grid?

We enjoy having our own opinion, so therefore, we must allow for others to have their beliefs as well. We used to call it common decency…which does not seem to be very common anymore.

Perhaps we should change the parameters of how we look at our purpose in life. Let us consider that our purpose has everything to do with this moment in history. That we are here, at this time specifically, for our purpose to manifest.

We all have things we enjoy and are good at, whether it is a sport at which we are particularly gifted, or a talent that is lauded. We may have fascinations with languages, sciences, or literature. Possibly we are inordinately artistic. It could well be that we will make tremendous contributions to the world with our abilities.

But what if our purpose in this life is to be happy and create for ourselves a heaven on earth? How would we go about ensuring that for ourselves?

Some people think the very basis of any happiness is having God in their lives, while some are the very opposite. It doesn't really matter. We are building our own model of how to live and how to enjoy life. The search for happiness can be a slippery slope. Just ask anyone. But heaven on earth? That is quite an order.

Let us first decide what heaven on earth would look and feel like? Since this is entirely individual all I can do is offer my personal view of it. I want joy in my life and lots of it! That would be my heaven.

Consider the possibility of a life of joy. What if our lives were filled with joy from morning until night? What if that joy was constant? Relish in that blissful thought.

Joy is something I much prefer over happiness. There is a difference, you know. Happiness comes from outside of oneself. Other people bring it to us, for example. Happiness enters our lives from enjoying events and things.

Joy, on the other hand, is attained once we make peace with ourselves and our place in the world. Joy is there when we find self-understanding and self-acceptance. When we find our authentic selves, and when begin to live in our own truth in this world…that is where joy is. And that makes the outside world, and whatever is going on in it, almost irrelevant.

If my life were filled to its brim with joy, it would not matter where I lived or who I lived with. All that I had would be enough.

My joy would manifest from my understanding of my place in the world, but I would also delight in knowing the Lord. The acceptance of His love and His grace would permeate my entire being. God's love would fulfill me, and I would, in turn, be able to radiate that love outward. I would, at that moment, have my own version of heaven on earth. Amen to it!

So rather than ask, why now, Lord? Perhaps we should think, why not now? We were born for this…

94

Spiritual Hunger

ಸಿಂಡ್

Being hungry is so much more than wanting or needing food for our bellies. Hunger can be needing nourishment for our minds and can also become a craving for our spirit to know God more completely. It is as if we need to eradicate the prolonged lack of knowledge and experience of God in our lives.

At a certain point in life the Bible stories from a childhood of Sunday School lessons, are just not fulfilling. Sunday services are unsatisfactory, and even meaningful discussions with other believers does not cut through the intensely strong desire to go beyond our mind's understanding of God's existence. We find ourselves eager to explore a different type of relationship with God. One that is filled with a loving awareness of His presence in our everyday lives. We feel a pull to fall in love with the Lord, and it is so strong that all we want to do is give back the love and then to give more.

The desire is to connect with not only the intensely creative and loving part of God, but to also touch the mystery of it all. It becomes the aspiration to live in the loving awareness of God's presence at all times. Some call this mysticism.

Mysticism is not about the occult, or weird charms or special powers. Mysticism simply goes beyond what the mind wonders and thinks about God. It takes religion and spirituality into the heart and to the very core of a person.

There is no specific roadmap to this mystical path. It is rather a result of one or many of life's events. Ultimately, one gains an understanding of how life works, our own human responsibility in all of it, and knowing that God is the basis of all things. Seeing the world in its entirety and our individual lives as precious gifts from God, makes us fall in love with our Creator.

Once one bravely opens to that deep abiding love, contemplating God's presence becomes second nature. One experiences God at the core of our being, and it is from this core that one sees and experiences all of life. It is the purest love. Having God at one's core does not interfere with the normal, human life, it simply enhances and improves it. This enriched inner core fills our souls with an understanding and peace that transcends the many difficulties that life has to offer and allows us the strength to carry on.

One of the many blessings from the Sermon on the Mount: Blessed are they which do hunger and thirst after righteousness: for they shall be filled. *(Matthew 5:6 KJV)*

95

You, Radical You!

☙❧

We all love to be inspired. Whether it be nature, the heavens at night or having a new experience, there is nothing like a new revelation. A new way to look at life that will stimulate and motivate us. Maybe it is the beauty of nature that draws us in, or our amazement at all the wonders that God fashioned. When a person that has inspired us, it is often because they are survivors of great trauma and unlimited pain. They have surpassed what we imagine we could possibly deal with, and we are moved by their strength, their endurance, their courage.

Many of us lead lives that others would envy. If we could only stop long enough to realize that while we are living our unendingly busy lives, we should be appreciating all that we do have already. Perhaps we would find that we have joy in our lives and would be ever so grateful for it. We could be appreciative for having a reliable car, rather than wishing we had a newer model. Grateful for the multitude of food choices we get to pick from every day. And how about the roof we have over our heads every night protecting us from the elements? Did we ever consider that the roof is something to be enthusiastically grateful about? Probably not if we have never experienced not having one. Imagine the miracle of being able to read and write and being able to communicate with each other. But how can we know to be thankful when we cannot conceive of life without the Internet or a smartphone in our pocket?

This, however, is not about being poor or about being rich. It is about being alive in the moment and knowing God. And it is about understanding that He loves the poor person without the roof and without the job just as much as He loves you and me. And really comprehending that. Understanding that concept completely can change your life.

We know God enough to want to experience more of Him. And to truly do that we have to let Him out of that small sacred space inside of us that we keep to ourselves. That deep covert place where we store away the truths we know about the Lord and dare not share for fear that our friends will not agree, nor will they like it. And then, heaven forbid, those friends will distance themselves from us because of our willingness to say something about our faith.

We look up to certain people for a reason. They may have achieved more in life than we have. They have homes and cars that we long to own. They have spouses and families we envy. They have achieved a status in the world that makes us envy them. They may be more daring risk takers.

We want to emulate what we see in them professionally or in the media. They have the lives we believe we want or should have. So, we keep pushing and striving and fighting for the bigger job, the better title. We crave the larger salary and the appearance of a better life. That is where the happiness is…out there…in the future. We are practically addicted to what has not yet happened. And we have no idea what lingers below that surface we so admire.

Do you know what radical means? When we think something is radical, we think of troublemakers and people with extreme views. We think fanatical, and way outside the normal box. But the truth is, radical really means getting to the root of something. Getting to the true origin.

So, let us get really radical and get to the root of our own spirituality. Let us get down into the depths inside ourselves and acknowledge the thoughts and questions we have about God. Thoughts that include what we believe and what we value in life. Let us bring out the opinions, the feelings and the judgments. Let us bring all this out in the open. Let us dare to speak of everything that has been concealed. What we are afraid of believing and of not believing. Let us rediscover what we were taught, compare it to the lives we now live, and see how it all measures up.

Is there love that is never completely shown? Not shown to us, our families, or to God? Are there questions that need to be asked and answered? Is there compassion that needs to be shown? Or forgiveness that needs the light of day?

Let us get radical with the origins of our spirituality and start practicing the very basics of our faith: to love one another. Let us experience the joy we know is hiding somewhere in our hearts. Let us shut out the external trappings of the world, and learn to dwell in the abiding love, compassion and joy of knowing God's love.

Better yet, let us be the most radical, and vocalize our beliefs. We will find a new audience, receptive to our joy in life, and they will find in us, inspiration.

96

What is Your Philosophy?

ஐଓ

Philosophers have been around since the beginning of time, and they come from all cultures and countries. These lovers of wisdom have had thoughts and opinions on every possible way of life. Hate to disappoint any burgeoning philosophers, but there is nothing new under the sun. We enjoy studying the Greeks, considered the founders of Western philosophy, and the Romans, or any number of others. The difference between those philosophies and us? How and what we personally experience in the world.

Though religion is most definitely a philosophy, philosophy is surely not a religion. Often, we grow up in a religion following our parents lead in spiritual practice. Should our parents have been extremely brave and come from different religions, we may be fortunate enough to have learned about both paths.

Philosophy is about studying reality and our existence. It is about the reason we do what we do each and every day. We determine what our experience is, and what choices we are going to make going forward. We do not go find a philosopher to see what they would do prior to making a decision.

In my opinion, practicing religion is a living philosophy, as it can be newly created every day. As such, religion can add an extra special layer to our lives. We can choose to study one, or we can choose to explore the gamut of them. We can try on different beliefs and spiritual choices to see what resonates with us. Finding folks who agree should not be difficult since we know there are thousands of religions out there.

Embracing spirituality generally is not something we explore and then give up. Rather it serves to open up a multitude of possibilities for our lives, and for our afterlife as well.

Accepting the sacredness of life not only opens our eyes to all the beauty in the world, but it also comes with hard challenges. To love the unlovable, and to forgive the unforgiveable. It can offer to us a life's worth of work, yet it is an inspired decision to make and to try.

Each new day is an opportunity to start on that path again with gratitude and a longing to find and feel the blessings that kind of life offers.

Whichever philosophy you choose to emulate or follow, may you find much success in your new or your continuing exploration. Find what resonates with you and choose. God loves you either way.

97

The Night is Magic

༄༅

I love sleep. There is no better feeling than waking up after eight or so hours of peaceful, restful, wonderful sleep. Sleep is the very best way to start my day. It brings out all the gratitude for that good night's sleep, and it certainly sets me up for my new day. Thank you, Lord, for the wakeup call this morning!

We do not really understand why sleep has been deemed necessary by our Creator, but we surely do need to engage in it regularly to be healthy.

Sleep's restorative powers are proven. Ask anyone who has ever suffered from sleep deficiency of any kind. During those sleepless nights, we are miserably tired and restless. We often cannot get comfortable enough to let the magic happen. Staying in bed does not help, and often neither does getting up. In the morning we feel we are running on empty with no perceptible energy remaining. We feel depleted, drained, and exhausted. We are not ourselves, but more like a cell phone quickly running out of juice.

Sleep is essentially a recovery period for us to top off our energy tanks. Sleep is good for the body, the mind, and the soul. Sleep renews our organs, bodily systems, and cells. Curling up in a comfy bed and drifting off to sleep unplugs us from our daily reality of busy, busy, busy. Not only does sleep reduce inflammation, but it also prepares our bodies to fight infection.

Our minds benefit as well because sleep de-stresses us. When we sleep, our brains can work on deeper processes, often working out our problems for us. As for our souls, getting good sleep grants us more of the ability to show compassion and to love. How you may wonder? Let us not forget that our bodies, minds, and souls work in conjunction with one another. With our bodies and minds interacting successfully and getting the rest that is needed, our stressors become limited. Our emotions are, in fact, in check and more balanced with good sleep.

As human beings we focus on our thoughts, our hearts, and the behaviors we exhibit to the world. But we need to also pay attention to what our bodies need. What they really need, in order to be fully functional. We do need more than those forty winks occasionally. We need complete rest and we need to sleep.

Perhaps sleep is God's reset button for us? Don't we use that method on all of our devices, turning them off for a bit before turning them on again?

Consider the possibility that God is saying to us with each new morning. You are reborn. It is time to awaken to a new world...a new you. The past is over. Get out there and make a difference in the world. This is the dawn of a new day for you to be compassionate...to be forgiving...to love... and to touch a heart.

98

True North

ಸಿಇ

Choice is what defines us as individuals. Our choices in life help us determine, often at an early age, what our true north is. A true north is a way of describing what we focus on in life: Our most deeply held beliefs, our values, and our principles. One might call it our inner compass.

We start making these decisions as soon as we come into the world. Our senses and our environment playing significant roles. Our earthly circumstances: economic situation, parental maturity both emotional and mental, and also the country, and the century we are born into. We make choices based on our observations and sensitivities to what we see and experience in the world we are presented. Where and how we experience happiness and joy. Were we frightened? Did we see and/or feel anger?

We form deep connections to people and things right from the start. There will always be experiences and feelings we will need to learn from, and perhaps work to overcome as adults. Always: no matter one's childhood. That is how life works. Rich or poor, or somewhere in between. Heathy parents or sickly ones. Parents that leave us at early ages or live very long lives. Addicts in the family. Siblings or no. Extended family, or not. Are we surrounded by emotional health? Physical health? Do we have homes or are we homeless? What kind of examples do we witness: generosity or greed? Did we find a silver spoon in our mouths, or must we beg and fight for each meal? Were we born into a spiritual or religious community? Obviously, the list just goes on and on.

And yet choice is the common ground. So very many choices to make. Survival is first, and how we fit into the families we have. As adults we become concerned about how we want to be perceived by others. Do we show that true self deep down inside ourselves, or do we mask it because we do not feel good enough, or simply that is not what we want others to see?

The circumstances we grew up in, may not be those we want to continue to live with. So, we choose a different way, a different path in life to survive and thrive. Are they always the best choices? Of course not. That is how we learn. Behold the failures of our lives, for they help to guide and influence the choices we do make in order to move forward.

Our inner compass has a direction it is following right now, whether we understand that to be true or not. That is the path that we are currently on. Whatever it is we have in our lives right now; we are working very hard for it to be so.

Don't like the path? Change course. We will have to work equally hard to change that direction as we have worked to get where we are now. But how?

Change our choices.

Easier said than done. Choices made in childhood cannot always be easily undone. Yet there is always a way through, around, or over the roadblocks we see in front of us. We have to see clearly what is blocking our way and seek the path forward. Seek it with our whole being.

How do we want to accomplish this? With love or with hate? With compassion or with disdain? With forgiveness or with blame. Choose. We must live our choices to our fullest ability. And we will succeed, for we have changed course into that new direction. Stay on that course, or not. Always our choice.

Having a choice is wonderful, yet we must learn and understand that having a choice entails many, many decisions along the way. It is not as simple as saying, "I want to be rich" or "I want to be loved." Changing our true north involves every decision. Striving to forgive those who have harmed us. Choosing to be a loving person. Choosing to live with integrity. It all plays together in one's life.

We are the culmination of every feeling, every reaction, and every experience of our entire lives to this point. This is an overwhelming truth. Take the time to grasp the concept. It is all a learning. It is a truth that will help us to comprehend why people do what they do and act the way they act.

There are many choices, many paths open to celebrating the Divine. Many of us settle for one focus, but there is a whole world out there that sees and feels differently. We may see God as the head of a religion, or as our Father or closest friend. Another may never want to use the word God, not because they don't see the beauty and wonder in this world, but they are more comfortable with the word Source, Great Spirit, or Mother Earth. That person has made a selection, a choice that suits their lives, their fears and joys, and their connection and contribution in life. Honor that as well.

Choice is fundamentally personal. It is how we create and control our individual reality. It may take different types of hard work to get where we desire to go. But it is our journey after all.

Whatever we may choose for our experiences here on Earth, whichever direction we may want our true north to be; we must do it with all of our heart, all of our soul, and all of our mind. Should we choose to love God, there is no other way to do it.

99

Cruising the River Denial

☙❧

Many of us have taken passage down this river, and probably more than one voyage. It is a lovely trip, and very protective to the traveler. To be sure, there are many reasons to make this type of journey: physical and emotional pain, fear, overwhelming stress, grief, and tragedy. Without a doubt, denial is psychologically very beneficial to us, as we use it both to protect ourselves personally and to shield us from greater trauma. It serves its purpose very well. Denial is the first coping mechanism we learn as children.

Denial gives us time to take a breath when something shocking or traumatic happens, or when we get so frightened, we feel paralyzed. We protect ourselves by refusing to accept the truth, because we need some time, maybe several days or weeks, to adjust to and process the pain. Coming to grips with what may be a new reality or challenges ahead is not always easy. In time, it is healthy to gradually accept the truth and deal with it.

Denial can have a dark side, and actually be dangerous when we refuse to acknowledge events and facts that we either witness or that come with overwhelming credible evidence.

Fear is a cruel master, and yet we allow it into our lives. We fear and deny our health issues, and any illness touching the lives of our loved ones. We dread any type of scary news, whether it is work related, involves addiction, or personal violence, and we will put off medical attention and mental help as long as we can get away with it. We suffer anxiety over financial problems, and we may cheat for money. We fear being alone, and therefore reject getting help with relationship conflicts. Terrorists are in the news often, and that makes us lose our sense of freedom.

Our personal world, as well as the global community have difficult situations for us to acknowledge, and denying the problems exist does not solve any of the concerns. In fact, it may well create greater issues when we completely ignore the truth.

So why bring talk about traumatic events and denial into this larger conversation about celebrating the Divine? Because this is the perfect place to put our fears, our trials, and our tribulations. It can be easy to forget we have a friend in Jesus. We must claim the privilege of praying to God and putting our beliefs and our hopes into action.

In our prayers we may say, Lord, take this burden from me. But we do not lay them at His feet and feel the relief of that release. We continue to carry the burdens and suffer more for it.

We have all heard that we should let go and let God. It is not just a saying, but it does require some action on our part to fulfill the promise God has given us.

Ultimately, this is all a matter of trust. Do we trust Him to protect, to guide, to take care of and love us? Do we trust that His love is unconditional? Do we believe His promises? We must put our beliefs into action, and when we do that, we can fully appreciate all His many blessings.

It is difficult enough to stop denying the facts of our lives, the often-painful realities of such. Yet if we can bravely name those fears and place them with our Creator for Him to handle, we will feel the blessing. That is just one of His many gifts to us. I would not want my burdens in anyone else's hands...would you?

100

Kintsugi

༨༩༨༨

Humans sometimes say they feel broken. A part of their lives has fallen apart and moving forward is painful or seemingly impossible. If this is happening to us, we can be consumed with what got us to this immovable place. The obstacle may be ours, or may belong to someone we love, because we also feel broken when we cannot fix someone else.

How do we start to feel whole again? How can we make our days less wracked with worry and concern, and change our nights back into what used to be peaceful sleep? We long for a magic wand to sweep the broken pieces into a distant past we no longer remember.

Yet there is something to be said for war wounds, and the battle scars of what we have already survived. If we are still here, we have truly survived what may have been the very worst period of our lives. It doesn't matter if they are physical, emotional or mental scratches, scrapes, or trauma...they are evidence of survival...of endurance...of persistence. A co-worker of mine once was so embarrassed by the scar running down her chest from heart surgery that had saved her life. She didn't have the perspective that she was a warrior and should be proud of that battle scar, as she had survived so much.

Perhaps we are 'perfectly broken' because we are designed to be that way. We are created in the image of God, and because we are human, we will always have faults. We will have emotions we do not know how to handle or how to show. We will have reactions we don't know how to control, and feelings some say we should not have. We may display our anxiety and pain in ways that are not socially acceptable. And then there are the medical issues and addictions that add to our struggles and pains.

Maybe we should look at what happens to us in life as part of our learning process that was created for us. We are to grow, and we are to learn, and hopefully heal and teach others a better way to be present in this world, therefore stopping the hurt and pain from being passed from generation to generation.

The process of living and learning and fixing ourselves often makes us incredibly beautiful human beings who just happen to have many memorable events happening in their lives. Who doesn't love a resurrection story???

Look at the Japanese art of Kintsugi where broken pottery is repaired by mending the cracked and broken areas with gold, silver, or platinum. This technique was not designed to hide the damaged areas, but to highlight them. This art, believed to have begun in the late 15th century, allowed for ceramic vessels to continue to stay in use, rather than be thrown away. The faulty areas were embraced and made to be part of the beauty of the object. That which was thought to be defective or broken, is actually incorporated and elevated.

Aren't humans worth valuing in this same way?

101

Open Sesame

☙❧

Reminiscent of how to access buried treasure, this saying is still used by those of us who first learned of it in the story of "Ali Baba and the Forty Thieves" in *One Thousand and One Nights*.[30] In the story, the phrase opens the mouth of a cave where treasure has been hidden. When the words are used now, it is not usually for the discovery of treasure, but to finally open a stuck door or the opening of an old box whose contents have long been forgotten. It is not a magic word, but the secret to revealing the treasure.

Treasure is often thought of as being lost and, therefore, needing to be rediscovered. Treasure meaning wealth and fortune, whether it be a hoard of food stores, gold and silver, or any of those items that bring something remarkable and precious out of the dark and into the light. Most of us think of treasure as something of monetary value.

But there are many types of treasure beyond jewels and golden calves. There are the riches of living a spiritual life, such as finding a peaceful existence in a raucous and wild 21st century. Perception is our reality, and as such, if we believe whole heartedly in anything, we will live in that perceived world despite what surrounds us.

Spiritual treasures include our being rich in faith, as

well as the mercy, love, and grace that the Lord provides. Many have heard of these treasures, yet believe they are unattainable. Understanding that these virtues are within reach is essential in finding them. The secret in finding these spiritual treasures begins with love.

One of the greatest treasures worth discovering is that life is an incomparable gift. Every single aspect of life is meant to be cherished. And right there is where many of us fail to grasp the entire concept. This profoundly precious gift, given to us by our Creator is not fully comprehended by us. We have constructed lures of money and power that have usurped our journey.

We take life for granted and are markedly upset when things don't go our way, or when someone we love becomes ill, let alone when someone dies. We blame God. We say why me, and subsequently decide we just don't need or trust Him anymore. We see all of it as unspeakable tragedy, and as far as God is concerned, unforgiveable that any misfortune should be happening to us. We may see it as God's anger with us.

We know of God. We pray. We show up in a church/synagogue/cathedral a few times a year. We may even say grace prior to a few meals. We want to know where the love is in all this that we were allegedly promised. But we can't see it or feel it, so we claim it doesn't exist.

It is the infinite love that created us that is unseen and undiscovered without the secret. The secret is love. But it is the kind of love that is emotional and felt with the whole of our being. It is the love that can only be found by practicing the aloneness of solitude, the tranquility of silence, and finding comfort in them.

Solitude itself offers so many benefits. It allows clear focus as it frees the mind. Practicing silence gets us out of our day-to-day demands for a while, whether they be technological or other stimulation. It is a refreshing break from the noise that bombards us constantly.

We need to practice solitude in order to find the peaceful

silence that produces a stillness within. Down where calm and peace reside within us. Hidden deep in the silence we find a place where we are willing to surrender.

In the surrender we relinquish earthly pain and suffering, and we offer ourselves up to the loving God. This surrender is not defeat, it is an opening of our hearts to the love that created everything...from the great, infinite universe, to the tiniest quarks that make up atoms.

This love is overwhelming and quite irresistible. It draws us into the tenderness we feel at the very depths of our souls. It engulfs our entire being, as we begin to grasp the intention that love is everything.

The affection is so intense that it creates true adoration and extreme gratitude for this thing called life. It is the treasure of finding the divine presence within our own hearts which has just been waiting to be realized. For it is truly not hidden at all. It is the fundamental truth of our existence, and once realized, will permeate our lives with the love and grace that has been bestowed upon us.

102

The Pursuit of Happiness

೫೧೧೫

The United States Declaration of Independence[31] has these well-known words in it. "We hold these truths to be self-evident, that all men are created equal, that they are endowed by their Creator with certain unalienable Rights, that among these are Life, Liberty and the pursuit of Happiness." Essentially this means the privilege to live free, and the entitlement to be happy.

In the late seventeen hundreds when the document was written, happiness was considered what God intended for us to have in our lives. How we enjoyed happiness was left it up to each of us to determine. Thomas Jefferson, the primary author of that document, declared those rights as undeniable and indisputable. So many years later and now many of us struggle to find happiness in our lives.

Did we go wrong somewhere in the last three hundred years? Was it the act of pursuing happiness that got us into trouble? Perhaps we just lost our way.

We know now that being happy is a choice, no matter our current circumstances. If we were to rewrite the Declaration today, would we change the 'pursuit of Happiness' to now read the pursuit of meaning or the quest to find our life's purpose? For that is now what we are told each individual needs to feel happy.

Happiness may still be what God intended, yet everything I read advises that He intended so much more for us.

A relationship with our Creator offers us not only unconditional love, but also grace. This aspect of Christianity ensures us that we will receive the Lord's blessings even though we do not deserve them. Grace is God's love in action consistently giving us His love and mercy.

With His love at the center of our lives, meaning and purpose fall right into place because He guides our way. In the context of this precious love, we get a completely different perspective of everything in life. Our entire environment transforms, as we feel the world around us with a heart bursting with tenderness and devotion...and eyes that long to show compassion to every soul.

It is the ultimate power of love. Surrender to it, and let it fill your life.

103

Full Embrace

☙❧

Knowing that our souls are eternal, and that they are created to be reflective of the deepest love, the purest harmony, and the most enduring peace is our goal. Entering this human life with physical bodies, we must learn how to not only use these forms, but also to survive with them in a world filled with much more than love, harmony, and peace.

Soul Gardening is how we find our way back to the authenticity of who we are at our core. The seeds of our truth are already there in our souls. We must choose to tend to those treasure filled kernels with loving kindness toward ourselves and others, in order for those seeds to germinate, and subsequently develop us into the whole of who we are meant to be as human beings. This nurturing helps us to establish strong roots by focusing the love, harmony, and peace on ourselves, and then watching ourselves blossom into our true selves.

We are surrounded by others making very different choices. Even if those folks are from the same city, belong to the same religious group, or are members of the same sex or race...we will not necessarily make the same choices in similar situations. It does not matter what we may share with another individual. We are unique. Our experiences as well as our interpretations differ. Even members of the same family are each on their own singular journeys.

It is for this reason that no other person in the world should have to make any decision or choice to satisfy us. The reverse is true as well. Ultimately our choices will take us down the path that we are meant to travel. We are exactly in life where we are meant to be right now. It is also true that some paths are more difficult to negotiate than others.

Some of us think that our enlightenment journey is taking too long. It takes as long as we allow it. Many of us have a lot to experience and to overcome. We all just need to learn to let go. We are all doing the very best we can each moment. That is a great lesson to learn for ourselves as well as understanding that of others. Mistakes along the path are not so much about the punishment as they should be about the growth that comes from navigating the particular path we are on.

None of us is perfect, and we will continue to be human for the rest of our lives. This makes seeking perfection a waste of time. Just do the best we are able to do. Accepting our humanness is another great lesson and will serve us well.

On this earthly journey we can live in any type of world we are willing to perceive. If we believe we live in a beautiful and loving world, we do. And we will see those qualities and have those experiences. As always it is our choice.

Believe there is a God or other loving source to our Universe or not. Always you are choosing. Whatever your choices may be, fully embrace them, and enjoy the ride. You may find that your closest and dearest friends are right there beside you with their arms in the air, loudly shouting with joy for more!

104

Shaping the Future

☙❧

What role do we play in shaping the future?

Some of us leave destinies behind. Generations in one profession or another. Businesses handed down from parent to child. Perhaps vocations easily adopted by willing and eager offspring. Some stress over how to divide inherited fortunes, while others hardly think about what to bequeath because they have little or nothing to leave. Either way each of us has left quite a legacy behind.

Our demeanor in every situation has been noticed. By those we love, and by those we do not. Our works have been noted, perhaps not by our God, but indeed by every earthly being we have met and/or have known on our journey here. If we have worked or belonged to any organization, we leave a legacy to any coworker who ever knew us.

Teachers leave a part of themselves with every student they ever attempt to educate. The same can be said of all nurses, doctors, and everyone serving others, in that they touch lives and leave each one with a legacy.

We are most concerned with what happens to our families and the friends we leave behind. Perhaps we have taken wonderful vacations together. Could be we loaned money that we never asked to be returned. Maybe we offered jobs to folks who really need a leg up.

Everyone will remember those good times, the generosity, and the extravagances. They may be the most memorable times of our lives.

But everyone will also remember how we behaved and what we said when confronted by the homeless person. The times when we missed the baseball game or the school play because of something we deemed higher on the 'need to do' list at the time.

The ones we care about will remember the times we drank too much, when we missed obligations by claiming to be ill when we weren't. Those cherished people will remember when and what we gave and when we did not. And that is not just money.

It is where and with whom we spent our precious time. When we were generous, and when we skimped or skipped out too. It is our very own feelings and thoughts about God that we demonstrate without lectures or speeches. For every one of those people know all the choices we made in this life. Each one of those folks know our hearts...very, very well.

When we think of legacies, we think of grand gestures. Leaving a legacy means that our lives mattered. That we mattered in the grand scheme of things. Our greatest legacy may well be our actions and interactions with others. How we treated those that have and those that have not.

Did we show kindness and understanding? Did we practice forgiveness? Did we show love and respect to every person and to all creatures? Did we walk away from things that would harm us? What have we taught those who look up to us?

Did we practice small gestures of kindness like paying a toll for the car behind us, or getting someone's coffee? How about holding a door open or paying a compliment? Is it a habit to say thank you and admit when we are wrong? Did we learn how important it is to not be busy every hour of the day? And to be of service? Did we realize others observed what shows and movies we watched, what books we read, and what kind of people we hung around?

Did we feel any wonder when we were out in nature? And the importance of continuing to learn throughout our lives? Were we curious about people and places? Did we love to travel? Were we excited to be alive? Did we smile a lot or at all? Did we know how to relax? Did we listen? Did we seek inspiration? Show gratitude? Did we find joy?

The most important inheritance we leave behind is one of character...especially when we think no one is looking. For when we touch another's life, and they learn from us to be kind, to be calm, or to give the benefit of the doubt, we have touched all the connections to, and the future generations of, that soul.

Now isn't that quite a legacy?

105

God Helps Those

☙☙

Many of you are already finishing the title with "who help themselves," and are unconsciously nodding your heads in agreement with the statement. This saying is attributed to Benjamin Franklin who wrote it in one of the issues of his *Poor Richard's Almamack*.[32] Eighteenth century America held onto our Puritan roots of reading and following the Bible. For the Puritan, this glorified God. For others, working hard and making money became the American dream. Many are still surprised to learn the phrase is not in the Bible.

Benjamin Franklin was a very successful man and led an incredibly interesting life. He was unusual in his religious practice, writing and following his own religious text. In the almanac he published, we learn of Franklin's thoughts on how to live, what to do about anger, hunger, fools, friendships, money and God, and many of his sayings are articulated to this day.

Doesn't the Bible teach us just the opposite of that saying though? Don't we actually find in the Bible that God helps the helpless? Wondering then, why we keep Franklin's saying alive? Is it that we have become judgmental enough to expect a person down on their luck to have done enough to satisfy us? That they have tried hard enough to deserve our help? What is enough?

It is not like we sit down with each homeless person we see and ask qualifying questions before handing them a few dollars. Ah, but I am sure we know of people who have not had a job in a while. Friends who need a hand with a mortgage payment. Cousins who used to have the world in their hands, and now are clamoring for a job. Still others who really never had much and are just barely keeping their heads above water. That's where our minds scramble for what we are supposed to do in those situations? Staying away is the easiest answer. The situation is muddled in our heads, and at all costs we want to avoid that kind of confusion.

Perhaps we decided early on that we would never lend money to friends. Family, we hoped, would never have to ask. We would do a little tithing, and we would give to charity. Besides there are agencies and churches to allot the monies out.

Okay.

Quick question. Have you ever asked God for a favor? A helping hand? A job? A boost when you were feeling down? Something for a friend perhaps?

What were your expectations? When you asked did you have hope in receiving something back? Did you believe your prayers would be answered?

What if it is God's wish that we be the answer to another's prayers? What if God is using us to facilitate another human being's life? What if our words are the comfort someone needs? What if a few bucks out of our pocket can alleviate someone else's suffering?

And it is not all about money. What if we were meant to teach someone how to love? Or how to hold their own against a bully? What if the person you are avoiding is here to teach you a lesson you could not learn otherwise?

What if?

Just be of assistance. Help out. Lend a hand. Comfort. Support. Rally round. Facilitate. Alleviate. Ameliorate.

The Talmud teaches us: Do not be daunted by the enormity of the world's grief. Do justly, now. Love mercy, now. Walk humbly, now. You are not obligated to complete the work, but neither are you free to abandon it.

106

Of Square Pegs and Round Holes

☙❧

The ability to hold God in our hearts, and at some point, fall in love with all the blessings of this life, is a treasure not everyone has found. It is not unusual to discover that our singular journey, really is just that.

Ultimately, we are all on the same path...just in very different places on it. That is a comforting thought, helping me when I struggle with the existence of so much suffering in the world.

One of my greatest joys as I listen for God's whispers, is when I realize that His hand is indeed at work in my life. He is there for me every day and every night. There are times when out of the blue it strikes me that He has just kept me safe from something or a miraculous event has just happened.

That is when I look up and say, "That was You, wasn't it?"

Laus Deo

www.SoulGardening.net

Endnotes

Scripture quotations from the King James Version (AV) unless stated otherwise.

1. Goldsmith, J. (1958). *Practicing the Presence: The Inspirational Guide to Regaining Meaning and a Sense of Purpose in Your Life.* New York: HarperCollins Publishers
2. "Just a Closer Walk with Thee" 1940. Arranged and published by Kenneth Morris
3. "Just as I Am" 1835. Written by Charlotte Elliott with music by William Batchelder Bradbury.
4. "How Great Thou Art" 1886. This song is the English translation by the Reverend Stuart K. Hine of the Swedish song, "O Store Gud," by the Rev. Carl Boberg.
5. "Softly and Tenderly" 1880. Written by Will L. Thompson
6. "Take My Hand, Precious Lord" (a.k.a. "Precious Lord, Take My Hand") is a gospel song from an 1844 tune. The lyrics were written by the Rev. Thomas A. Dorsey, who also adapted the melody. Earliest known recording was in 1937.
7. https://en.wikipedia.org/wiki/Ichthys This page was last edited on 28 October 2019, at 13:17 (UTC). Information pulled November 16, 2019. Wikipedia® is a registered trademark of the Wikimedia Foundation, Inc., a non-profit organization.
8. https://en.wikipedia.org/wiki/Sign_of_the_Dove This page was last edited on 4 October 2019, at 05:25 (UTC). Information pulled November 16, 2019. Wikipedia® is a registered trademark of the Wikimedia Foundation, Inc., a non-profit organization.
9. https://en.wikipedia.org/wiki/Celtic_cross This page was last edited on 11 November 2019, at 21:38 (UTC). Information pulled November 16, 2019. Wikipedia® is a registered trademark of the Wikimedia Foundation, Inc., a non-profit organization.

10. 'Jesus Christ Superstar,' the 1970 rock opera with music by Andrew Lloyd Webber and lyrics by Tim Rice made its Broadway debut in 1971.
11. As example of a song with lyrics that can be interpreted as a relationship with the Lord is: "Dark Night of the Soul – St. John of the Cross" by Lorena McKennitt as part of her 1994 album *The Mask and Mirror*, published by Quinlan Road.
12. Permission to reprint this rendering of the Lord's Prayer from the Aramaic by Mark Hathaway, graciously provided by Mark Hathaway with an acknowledgment this draws on the work of Neil Douglas-Klotz. Websites: www.taoofiberation.com and www.abwoon.com
13. https://en.wikipedia.org/wiki/Krishna This page was last edited on 16 November 2019, at 13:23 (UTC). Information pulled November 16, 2019. Wikipedia® is a registered trademark of the Wikimedia Foundation, Inc., a non-profit organization.
14. https://en.wikipedia.org/wiki/Zoroaster This page was last edited on 5 November 2019, at 18:58 (UTC). Information pulled November 16, 2019. Wikipedia® is a registered trademark of the Wikimedia Foundation, Inc., a non-profit organization.
15. https://en.wikipedia.org/wiki/Confucius This page was last edited on 15 November 2019, at 09:35 (UTC). Information pulled November 16, 2019. Wikipedia® is a registered trademark of the Wikimedia Foundation, Inc., a non-profit organization.
16. https://en.wikipedia.org/wiki/Gautama_Buddha This page was last edited on 13 November 2019, at 15:39 (UTC). Information pulled November 16, 2019. Wikipedia® is a registered trademark of the Wikimedia Foundation, Inc., a non-profit organization.
17. https://en.wikipedia.org/wiki/Socrates This page was last edited on 11 November 2019, at 08:49 (UTC). Information pulled November 16, 2019. Wikipedia® is a registered trademark of the Wikimedia Foundation, Inc., a non-profit organization.

18 https://en.wikipedia.org/wiki/Bah%C3%A1%27%C3%AD_Faith This page was last edited on 14 November 2019, at 11:08 (UTC). Information pulled November 16, 2019. Wikipedia® is a registered trademark of the Wikimedia Foundation, Inc., a non-profit organization.
19 Drosnin, Michael. (1997). *The Bible Code*. Ojai: Atria Books
20 Edited by Rodolphe Kasser, Marvin Meyer, and Gregor Wurst in collaboration with François Gaudard. (2006). *The Gospel of Judas from Codex Tchacos*. Washington: National Geographic
21 "Joy to the World"
Written by Isaac Watts in 1719 and based on Psalm 98 and Genesis 3.
22 https://en.wikipedia.org/wiki/Constantine_the_Great This page was last edited on 12 November 2019, at 15:22 (UTC). Information pulled November 16, 2019. Wikipedia® is a registered trademark of the Wikimedia Foundation, Inc., a non-profit organization.
23 "O Holy Night" 1847.
Adolphe Charles Adam was a French composer, 1803 to 1856. He created a Christmas carol from "Minuit, Cretiéns", which was later set to different English lyrics and sung as "O Holy Night" in 1847.
24 "I Surrender All" 1896. Judson W. Van DeVenter
25 https://en.wikipedia.org/wiki/Kojak This page was last edited on 20 October 2019, at 02:42 (UTC). Information pulled November 16, 2019. Wikipedia® is a registered trademark of the Wikimedia Foundation, Inc., a non-profit organization.
26 "Just as I Am" 1835. Written by Charlotte Elliott with music by William Batchelder Bradbury.
27 Williams, M. (1922). *The Velveteen Rabbit*. New York. George H. Doran Company
28 https://en.wikipedia.org/wiki/Easter This page was last edited on 10 November 2019, at 09:07 (UTC). Information pulled November 16, 2019. Wikipedia® is a registered trademark of the Wikimedia Foundation, Inc., a non-profit organization.

29 "Oh Happy Day" by Philip Doddridge. 18th century.
30 Galland, A & Mahdi, M. (1704). *One Thousand and One Nights*. Published in the Middle East.
31 https://en.wikipedia.org/wiki/United_States_Declaration_of_Independence. This page was last edited on 8 November 2019, at 21:15 (UTC). Information pulled November 16, 2019. Wikipedia® is a registered trademark of the Wikimedia Foundation, Inc., a non-profit organization.
32 https://en.wikipedia.org/wiki/Poor_Richard's_Almanack This page was last edited on 9 November 2019, at 07:30 (UTC). Information pulled November 16, 2019. Wikipedia® is a registered trademark of the Wikimedia Foundation, Inc., a non-profit organization.

CPSIA information can be obtained
at www.ICGtesting.com
Printed in the USA
LVHW030335221220
674783LV00001B/52